Anarchism: A Very Short Introduction

...UCTIONS are for anyone wanting a stimulating
... to a new subject. They are written by experts, and have
... more than 25 languages worldwide.
... began in 1995, and now represents a wide variety of topics
... philosophy, religion, science, and the humanities. Over the next
... s it will grow to a library of around 200 volumes – a Very Short
Introduction to everything from ancient Egypt and Indian philosophy to
conceptual art and cosmology.

Very Short Introductions available now:

Available soon:

AFRICAN HISTORY
  John Parker and Richard Rathbone
THE BRAIN   Michael O'Shea
BUDDHIST ETHICS
  Damien Keown
CHAOS   Leonard Smith
CHRISTIANITY   Linda Woodhead
CITIZENSHIP   Richard Bellamy
CLASSICAL ARCHITECTURE
  Robert Tavernor
CLONING   Arlene Judith Klotzko
CONSCIOUSNESS
  Sue Blackmore
CONTEMPORARY ART
  Julian Stallabrass
THE CRUSADES
  Christopher Tyerman
DERRIDA   Simon Glendinning
DESIGN   John Heskett
DINOSAURS   David Norman
DREAMING   J. Allan Hobson
ECONOMICS   Partha Dasgupta
THE ELEMENTS   Philip Ball
THE END OF THE WORLD
  Bill McGuire
EXISTENTIALISM   Thomas Flynn
FEMINISM   Margaret Walters
THE FIRST WORLD WAR
  Michael Howard

FOUCAULT   Garry Gutting
FUNDAMENTALISM
  Malise Ruthven
HABERMAS   Gordon Finlayson
HIROSHIMA   B. R. Tomlinson
HUMAN EVOLUTION
  Bernard Wood
INTERNATIONAL RELATIONS
  Paul Wilkinson
JAZZ   Brian Morton
MANDELA   Tom Lodge
THE MIND   Martin Davies
MODERN ART   David Cottington
NATIONALISM   Steven Grosby
PERCEPTION   Richard Gregory
PHILOSOPHY OF RELIGION
  Jack Copeland and Diane Proudfoot
PHOTOGRAPHY   Steve Edwards
THE RAJ   Denis Judd
THE RENAISSANCE
  Jerry Brotton
RENAISSANCE ART
  Geraldine Johnson
THE ROMAN EMPIRE
  Christopher Kelley
SARTRE   Christina Howells
THE SPANISH CIVIL WAR
  Helen Graham
TRAGEDY   Adrian Poole

For more information visit our web site
www.oup.co.uk/vsi

Colin Ward

ANARCHISM

A Very Short Introduction

OXFORD
UNIVERSITY PRESS

OXFORD

UNIVERSITY PRESS

Great Clarendon Street, Oxford OX2 6DP

Oxford University Press is a department of the University of Oxford.
It furthers the University's objective of excellence in research, scholarship,
and education by publishing worldwide in

Oxford New York

Auckland Bangkok Buenos Aires Cape Town Chennai
Dar es Salaam Delhi Hong Kong Istanbul Karachi Kolkata
Kuala Lumpur Madrid Melbourne Mexico City Mumbai Nairobi
São Paulo Shanghai Taipei Tokyo Toronto

Oxford is a registered trade mark of Oxford University Press
in the UK and in certain other countries

Published in the United States
by Oxford University Press Inc., New York

British Library Cataloguing in Publication Data

Data available

Library of Congress Cataloging in Publication Data

Ward, Colin.
Anarchism: a very short introduction / Colin Ward.
p. cm.—(Very short introductions ; 116)
Includes bibliographical references and index.
ISBN 0-19-280477-4 (pbk. : alk. paper)
1. Anarchism. 2. Anarchism—History. I. Title. II. Series.
HX833.W36 2004 335′.83—dc22 2004013626

ISBN 0-19-280477-4

1 3 5 7 9 10 8 6 4 2

Typeset by RefineCatch Ltd, Bungay, Suffolk
Printed in Great Britain by
TJ International Ltd, Padstow, Cornwall

Contents

Foreword

Anarchism is a social and political ideology which, despite a history of defeat, continually re-emerges in a new guise or in a new country, so that another chapter has to be added to its chronology, or another dimension to its scope.

In 1962 George Woodcock wrote a 470-page book, *Anarchism*, which, continually reprinted as a Penguin Book and translated into many languages, became probably the most widely read book on the subject in the world. Woodcock wrote a series of updating postscripts until his death in 1995.

In 1992 Peter Marshall wrote a book of more than 700 pages called *Demanding the Impossible: A History of Anarchism* (HarperCollins) which seems likely to overtake the earlier book in global sales. Woodcock was greatly relieved: 'I now have a book,' he wrote, 'to which I can direct readers when they ask me how soon I intend to bring my *Anarchism* up to date.' Like all his other readers, I have been very grateful for Peter Marshall's capacity for summarizing complex ideas and for exploring the by-ways of anarchist history.

For decades, when in search of a fact or an opinion, I would telephone Nicolas Walter, who died in the year 2000. I greatly value his neat little pamphlet *About Anarchism*, which is part of the global treasury of anarchist literature stocked by the Freedom Press Bookshop in London.

My task has been one of selection: simply an attempt to introduce the reader to anarchist ideas in a very few words and to point to further sources. In this rich field the emphases are bound to be my own.

C. W.

February 2004

List of illustrations

Chapter 1
Definitions and ancestors

The word 'anarchy' comes from the Greek *anarkhia*, meaning contrary to authority or without a ruler, and was used in a derogatory sense until 1840, when it was adopted by Pierre-Joseph Proudhon to describe his political and social ideology. Proudhon argued that organization without government was both possible and desirable. In the evolution of political ideas, anarchism can be seen as an ultimate projection of both liberalism and socialism, and the differing strands of anarchist thought can be related to their emphasis on one or the other of these.

Historically, anarchism arose not only as an explanation of the gulf between the rich and the poor in any community, and of the reason why the poor have been obliged to fight for their share of a common inheritance, but as a radical answer to the question 'What went wrong?' that followed the ultimate outcome of the French Revolution. It had ended not only with a reign of terror and the emergence of a newly rich ruling caste, but with a new adored emperor, Napoleon Bonaparte, strutting through his conquered territories.

The anarchists and their precursors were unique on the political Left in affirming that workers and peasants, grasping the chance that arose to bring an end to centuries of exploitation and tyranny, were inevitably betrayed by the new class of politicians, whose first priority was to re-establish a centralized state power. After every revolutionary uprising, usually won at a heavy cost for ordinary populations, the new rulers had no hesitation in applying violence and terror, a secret police, and a professional army to maintain their control.

For anarchists the state itself is the enemy, and they have applied the same interpretation to the outcome of every revolution of the 19th and 20th centuries. This is not merely because every state keeps a watchful and sometimes punitive eye on its dissidents, but because every state protects the privileges of the powerful.

The mainstream of anarchist propaganda for more than a century has been *anarchist-communism*, which argues that property in land, natural resources, and the means of production should be held in mutual control by local communities, federating for innumerable joint purposes with other communes. It differs from state socialism in opposing the concept of any central authority. Some anarchists prefer to distinguish between anarchist-communism and *collectivist anarchism* in order to stress the obviously desirable freedom of an individual or family to possess the resources needed for living, while not implying the right to own the resources needed by others.

Anarcho-syndicalism puts its emphasis on the organized industrial workers who could, through a 'social general strike', expropriate the possessors of capital and thus engineer a workers' take-over of industry and administration.

There are, unsurprisingly, several traditions of *individualist anarchism*, one of them deriving from the 'conscious egoism' of the German writer Max Stirner (1806–56), and another from a remarkable series of 19th-century American figures who argued that in protecting our own autonomy and associating with others for common advantages, we are promoting the good of all. These thinkers differed from free-market liberals in their absolute mistrust of American capitalism, and in their emphasis on mutualism. In the late 20th century the word 'libertarian', which people holding such a viewpoint had previously used as an alternative to the word 'anarchist', was appropriated by a new group of American thinkers, who are discussed in Chapter 7.

Pacifist anarchism follows both from the anti-militarism that accompanies rejection of the state, with its ultimate dependence on armed forces, and from the conviction that any morally viable human society depends upon the uncoerced goodwill of its members.

These and other threads of anarchist thought have different emphases. What links them all is their rejection of external authority, whether that of the state, the employer, or the hierarchies of administration and of established institutions like the school and the church. The same is true of more recently emerging varieties of anarchist propaganda, *green anarchism* and *anarcha-feminism*. Like those who believe that animal liberation is an aspect of human liberation, they claim that the only ideology consistent with their aims is anarchism.

It is customary to relate the anarchist tradition to four major thinkers and writers. The first was William Godwin (1756–1836), who in his *Enquiry Concerning Political Justice*, published in 1793, set out the anarchist case against government, the law, property, and the institutions of the state. He was the partner of Mary Wollstonecraft and the father of Mary Shelley, and was an heir of both the English tradition of radical nonconformity and of the French *philosophes*. His book brought him instant fame, soon followed by hostility and neglect in the political climate of the early 19th century, but it had an underground life in radical circles until its rediscovery by the anarchist movement in the 1890s.

The second of these pioneers was Pierre-Joseph Proudhon (1809–65), the French propagandist who was the first one to call

1. **William Godwin (1756–1836), from the portrait by James Northcote, now in the National Portrait Gallery, London.**

himself an anarchist. He became famous in 1840 by virtue of an essay that declared that 'Property is Theft', but he also claimed that 'Property is Freedom'. He saw no contradiction between these two slogans, since he thought it obvious that the first related to the landowner and capitalist whose ownership derived from conquest or exploitation and was sustained only through the state, its property laws, police, and army; while the second was concerned with the peasant or artisan family with an obvious natural right to a home, to the land it could cultivate, and to the tools of a trade, but not to ownership or control of the homes, land, or livelihood of others. Proudhon was criticized for being a mere survivor of the world of peasant farmers and small artisans in local communities, but he had a ready response in setting out the principles of successful federation.

The third of the classical anarchist luminaries was the Russian revolutionary Michael Bakunin (1814–76), deservedly famous for his disputes with Marx in the First International in the 1870s, where, for his successors, he predicted with remarkable accuracy the outcome of Marxist dictatorships in the 20th century. 'Freedom without socialism,' he said, 'is privilege and injustice, but socialism without freedom is slavery and brutality.' His elaborations on this perception are cited in innumerable books published since the collapse of the Soviet Union, and subsequently of the regimes it imposed on its satellites. Typical of Bakunin's observations was a letter of 1872 in which he remarked:

> I believe that Herr Marx is a very serious if not very honest revolutionary, and that he really is in favour of the rebellion of the masses, and I wonder how he manages to overlook the fact that the establishment of a universal dictatorship, collective or individual, a dictatorship which would create the post of a kind of chief engineer of world revolution, ruling and controlling the insurrectionary activity of the masses in all countries, as a machine might be controlled – that the establishment of such a dictatorship would in itself suffice to kill revolution and warp and paralyse all popular movements . . .

The last of these key thinkers was another Russian of aristocratic origin, Peter Kropotkin (1842–1921). His original reputation derived from his work as a geographer, and in a long series of books and pamphlets he sought to give anarchism a scientific basis. *The Conquest of Bread* (1892) was his manual on the

2. Pierre-Joseph Proudhon (1809–65), from the painting of *Proudhon and His Children* (1865) by Gustave Courbet.

3. **Michael Bakunin (1814–76), an early portrait.**

self-organization of a post-revolutionary society. *Mutual Aid* (1902) was written to confront those misinterpretations of Darwinism that justified competitive capitalism, by demonstrating from the observation of animal and human societies that competition within species is far less significant than cooperation as a precondition for survival.

Fields, Factories and Workshops (1899) was Kropotkin's treatise on the humanization of work, through the integration of agriculture and industry, of brain work and physical work, and of intellectual and manual education. The most widely read on a global scale of all anarchist authors, he linked anarchism both with subsequent ideas of social ecology and with everyday experience.

Some anarchists would object to the identification of anarchism with its best-known writers. They would point out that everywhere in the world where anarchist ideas have arisen, there is a local activist conspiring to get access to a printing press, aware of the anarchist undercurrent in every uprising of the downtrodden all through history, and full of ideas about the application of anarchist solutions to local issues and dilemmas. They point to the way in which anarchist aspirations can be traced through the slave revolts of the ancient world, the peasant risings of medieval Europe, in the aims of the Diggers in the English Revolution of the 1640s, in the revolutions in France in 1789 and 1848, and the Paris Commune of 1871. In the 20th century, anarchism had a role in the Mexican Revolution of 1911, the Russian Revolution of 1917, and most notably in the revolution in Spain that followed the military uprising that precipitated the civil war in 1936. The part played by the anarchists in these revolutionary situations is described in the following chapter.

In all these revolutions the fate of the anarchists was that of heroic losers. But anarchists do not necessarily fit the stereotype of believers in some ultimate revolution, succeeding where all others had failed, and inaugurating Utopia. The German anarchist Gustav Landauer declared that:

> The state is not something which can be destroyed by a revolution, but is a condition, a certain relationship between human beings, a mode of human behaviour; we destroy it by contracting other relationships, by behaving differently.

4. Peter Kropotkin (1842–1921) photographed in 1864, the year of his first explorations of unmapped regions of Siberia.

Moreover, if the anarchists have not changed society in the ways that they hoped were possible, the same is true for the advocates of every other social ideology of the past century, whether socialist or capitalist. But, as I stress in Chapter 8, they have contributed to a long series of small liberations that have lifted a huge load of human misery.

Anarchism has, in fact, an enduring resilience. Every European, North American, Latin American, and Asian society has had its anarchist publicists, journals, circles of adherents, imprisoned activists, and martyrs. Whenever an authoritarian and repressive political regime collapses, the anarchists are there, a minority urging their fellow citizens to absorb the lessons of the sheer horror and irresponsibility of government.

The anarchist press re-emerged in Germany after Hitler, in Italy after Mussolini, in Spain after Franco, in Portugal after Salazar, in Argentina after the generals, and in Russia after 70 years of brutal suppression. For anarchists this is an indication that the ideal of a self-organizing society based on voluntary cooperation rather than upon coercion is irrepressible. It represents, they claim, a universal human aspiration. This is illustrated by the way that people from non-European cultures took Western anarchist ideas and concepts and linked them to traditions and thinkers from their own countries.

Anarchist ideas were brought to Japan by Kotuku Shusui in the very early years of the 20th century. He had read Kropotkin's writings while in prison during the Russo-Japanese War of 1904–5. When released he visited California, making contact with the militant anarcho-syndicalists of the Industrial Workers of the World (IWW), and returned to Japan to publish an anti-militarist journal, *Heimen*. Kotuku claimed that there was always an anarchist undercurrent in Japanese life, deriving from both Buddhism and Taoism. He was one of 12 anarchists executed in 1911, accused of plotting against the Emperor Meiji. All through the first half of the century, a series of successors continued propaganda and industrial action against militarism, and were suppressed by government, to reappear in a changed climate after the horrors of the Second World War.

Chinese anarchism emerged at much the same time, through the influence of students who had been to Tokyo or to Paris. Those who studied in Japan were influenced by Kotuku Shusui, and stressed the links with a long-established stream in Chinese life. As Peter Marshall explains,

> Modern anarchism not only advocated the Taoist rural idyll, but also echoed the peasant longing embedded in Chinese culture for a frugal and egalitarian millennium which had expressed itself in peasant rebellions throughout Chinese history. It further struck a chord with two traditional concepts, *Ta-t'ung*, a legendary golden age of social equality and harmony, and *Ching-t'ien*, a system of communal land tenure.

Those young Chinese who studied in Paris were attracted by the writings of Bakunin and Kropotkin, as well as by Darwinian evolutionary theory. They rejected attempts to link anarchism with Lao Tzu's Taoism and with agrarian history. With the fall of the Manchu dynasty in 1911, both anarchist factions thought that their hour had come. But in fact the revolutionary ideology that slowly triumphed in the turbulent history of 20th-century China was that of the Marxist-Leninists. And as we shall see in Chapter 2, the programmes imposed by force on the Chinese were a dictatorial parody of anarchist aspirations.

Korea, too, has an anarchist tradition linked with 19th-century hopes for peasant communism, but due to 35 years of Japanese occupation fiercely resisted by the anarchists, among other political factions, their reputation is that of patriots in a country where the North is a Marxist dictatorship while the South is a model of American-style capitalism.

In India the history of the first half of the 20th century, and the struggle to end British rule, was dominated by Mohandas K. Gandhi, who built a unique ideology of non-violent resistance and peasant socialism from a series of semi-anarchist sources and linked them with Indian traditions. From Tolstoy he evolved his policy of non-violent resistance, from Thoreau he took his philosophy of civil disobedience, and from a close reading of Kropotkin his programme of decentralized and autonomous village communes linking agriculture with local industry. After independence was achieved, his political successors revered his memory but ignored his ideas. Later in the century Vinoba Bhave's *Sarvodaya* movement sought a non-violent land-based revolution, rejecting the politics of central government.

In Africa, Mbah and Igarewey the authors of a study of the failure of state socialism imposed by governments draw attention to the

seemingly endemic problem of ethnic conflicts across the continent; the continued political and economic marginalization of Africa at the global level; the unspeakable misery of about 90 per cent of Africa's population; and, indeed, the ongoing collapse of the nation state in many parts of Africa.

They argue that:

Given these problems, a return to the 'anarchic elements' in African communalism is virtually inevitable. The goal of a self-managed society born out of the free will of its people and devoid of authoritarian control and regimentation is as attractive as it is feasible in the long run.

The reader may wonder why, if ideas and aspirations similar to those of the anarchists can be traced through so many cultures around the world, the concept is so regularly misunderstood or caricatured. The answer is to be found in a very small episode in anarchist history.

There was a period, a century ago, when a minority of anarchists, like the subsequent minorities of a dozen other political movements, believed that the assassination of monarchs, princes, and presidents would hasten popular revolution. Sad to say, the most deserving victims, Mussolini, Franco, Hitler, or Stalin, were well protected, and in terms of changing the course of history and ridding the world of its tyrants the anarchists were no more successful than most subsequent political assassins. But their legacy has been the cartoonist's stereotype of the anarchist as the cloaked and bearded carrier of a spherical bomb with a smoking fuse, and this has consequently provided yet another obstacle to the serious discussion of anarchist approaches. Meanwhile, modern political terrorism on an indiscriminate scale is the monopoly of governments and is directed at civilian populations, or is the weapon we all associate with religious or nationalist separatism, both of them very far from the aspirations of anarchists.

In the entry for 'Anarchism' that Kropotkin wrote in 1905 for the 11th edition of the *Encyclopaedia Britannica*, he began by explaining that it is

> the name given to a principle or theory of life and conduct under which society is conceived without government – harmony in such a society being obtained, not by submission to law, or by obedience to any authority, but by free agreements, concluded between the various groups, territorial and professional, freely constituted for the sake of production and consumption, as also for the satisfaction of the infinite variety of needs and aspirations of a civilised being.

Implicit in this definition is the inevitability of compromise, an ordinary aspect of politics which has been found difficult by anarchists, precisely because their ideology precludes the usual routes to political influence.

Chapter 2
Revolutionary moments

In the course of the revolutionary outbreaks that spread across Europe in 1848 the Prefect of Police in Paris is said to have remarked of the anarchist Michael Bakunin, 'What a man! On the first day of the revolution he is a perfect treasure; but on the next day he ought to be shot.' His observation epitomizes both the role and the ultimate fate of the anarchists and their precursors in a long series of European popular uprisings.

Chroniclers of all political movements invariably discover antecedents from the past, and the anarchists found ancestors in the slave revolts of the Roman Empire and in all subsequent revolutionary upheavals of the downtrodden. They have similarly identified precursors in such risings as the Peasants' Revolt that began in England in 1391, in the insurrection of the Taborites in Bohemia in 1493 and that of the Anabaptists a century later.

In the English Revolution of the civil war years leading up to 1649, the anarchist element was illustrated by the activities of the Diggers, Ranters, and Levellers, who, having helped to ensure Cromwell's success, were described by one pamphleteer as 'Switzerising anarchists' and were rapidly eliminated once the Protector was securely in power, only to be followed by the eventual return of the monarchy. But the people who dared to remove a king had opened the way to more radical thoughts on the relationship between the individual and the community and between society and the state. The American and French revolutions of the following century brought a message beautifully expressed in Thomas Paine's *Common Sense* in 1776:

> Society in every state is a blessing, but government even in its best state is but a necessary evil; in its worst state an intolerable one; for when we suffer, or are exposed to the same miseries by a *government* which we might expect in a country *without a government*, our calamity is heightened by reflecting that we furnish the means by which we suffer. Government, like dress, is the badge of lost innocence: the palaces of kings are built on the ruins of the bowers of paradise.

Political ideas crossed the Atlantic almost as rapidly in the 18th century as in the 21st, and the American Revolution made the French Revolution inevitable. Jefferson, Paine, and Franklin had a role in both, while William Godwin in his *Enquiry Concerning Political Justice* was arguing the anarchist case from first principles. Meanwhile, a series of brave opponents of the new French state, known as the *Enragés* and gathered around Jacques Roux and Jean Varlet, opposed the new rulers. Varlet, who actually survived the Terror, observed that

> Despotism has passed from the palace of kings to the circle of a committee. It is neither the royal robes, nor the sceptre, nor the crown, that makes kings hated, but ambition and tyranny. In my country there has been only a change in dress.

Anarchism reappeared in the European revolutions of 1848. In the following year, after the failure of the revolution in Dresden, Bakunin was imprisoned, condemned to death, and after a year handed over to the Austrians, condemned again, but in the next year handed over to the Russians. After six years in the Peter-and-Paul fortress at St Petersburg he was exiled to Siberia, whence he eventually escaped to London by way of Japan, San

Francisco, and New York. After the Franco-Prussian War of 1870, Proudhon's federalist ideas shaped the short-lived Paris Commune and its 'Manifesto to the French People' of April 1871, which urged:

> The absolute autonomy of the Commune extended to all the localities of France, assuring to each its integral rights and to every Frenchman the full exercise of his aptitudes, as a man, a citizen, and a worker. The autonomy of the Commune will have for its limits only the equal autonomy of all other communities adhering to the contract; their association must assure the liberty of France.

(Needless to say, although the Commune had an admired anarchist heroine, Louise Michel, its Manifesto did not extend these rights to Frenchwomen.)

In the major revolutions of the 20th century there were recognizable anarchist elements, but in each of them the anarchists were victims of the new rulers. In Mexico, Ricardo Flores Magon and his brothers had in 1900 begun publication of an anarcho-syndicalist newspaper *Regeneración*, building up opposition to the dictator Porfirio Diaz, slipping across the border into California when publication became too difficult. With the fall of Diaz, Magon established contact with the peasant revolutionary Emiliano Zapata in the state of Morales in the South, fighting the efforts of large landowners to annex the land of poor growers. Magon is said to have made Zapata literate through reading and discussing Kropotkin's *The Conquest of Bread*. Zapata was ambushed and killed in 1919, while Magon was jailed in the United States and was murdered in Leavenworth Penitentiary in 1923. Ironically, both men are celebrated in the Rotunda of Illustrious Men in Mexico City. The contemporary EZLN (Zapatista Army of National Liberation) is Mexico's modern incarnation of Zapata's campaign, as is, for example, the MST (Movement of Landless Rural Workers) in Brazil. Both of these are campaigns of dispossessed peasants for communal control of land seized by large-scale cattle-ranching oligarchies.

5. In Chiapas, Mexico's southernmost and, in 2003, poorest state, a Tzotzil Indian woman walks past a notice proclaiming that 'You are in Zapatista territory. Here the people rule and the government obeys.'

6. Emiliano Zapata and Pancho Villa riding into Mexico City in 1914, having driven out General Huerta. Zapata himself was ambushed and killed in 1919.

In the Russian Revolution of 1917 the Bolshevik seizure of power was pushed through with anarchist slogans like 'Bread and Freedom' and 'All Power to the Soviets', which were very far from daily experience in the new regime. The anarchist hero of the revolution was the Ukrainian peasant Nestor Makhno, organizing peasant land seizures and defending them from both the Bolsheviks and the Whites. Returning Russian exiles included Emma Goldman and Alexander Berkman, deported from the United States, and Kropotkin, who had been obliged to live abroad for 40 years. Kropotkin addressed critical letters to Lenin and wrote a *Letter to the Workers of Western Europe* describing for them the lessons of the Russian Revolution. His funeral in 1921 was the last occasion when the Russian anarchists were at liberty until the slow releases from Stalin's prison camps after 1956.

Goldman and Berkman tried to tell the truth about Lenin's Russia when they left the country, but found that the political Left in the

7. The burial of Kropotkin in Moscow in 1921. It is said that the anarchists were released from prison for one day to attend this occasion. The speaker in this picture is Emma Goldman, and below her is Alexander Berkman.

West rejected their message, seeing it as 'counter-revolutionary'. The same kind of exclusion by the political Left faced continual anarchist attempts to reveal the truth about the Soviet Union, while Stalinist infiltration destroyed the integrity of a long series of workers' organizations in the West.

Italy's anarchist tradition began when Bakunin settled there in 1863, recommended to fellow revolutionaries by Garibaldi and Mazzini, whose nationalism he actually opposed in the name of communal autonomy and federalism. To this period of Bakunin's life belong his polemics against Marx which, accurately and uniquely, foresaw the evolution of Marxist dictatorships in the 20th century. His disciple Errico Malatesta, who died under house arrest in Mussolini's Italy, initiated streams of anarchist propaganda in Italy and Latin America, which still flow to this day in the form of an impressive spread of publications and campaigns.

In the Far East, the habit of sending young men from affluent families to complete their education in Europe led to a string of revolutionary students bringing back to China from Paris the anarchist message of Kropotkin in his propagandist books *The Conquest of Bread*, *Mutual Aid*, and especially *Fields, Factories and Workshops*. Many of the shifts and turns of Communist Party policy in China in the 1950s and 1960s have recognizable links with Kropotkin's agenda, although, of course, they were imposed with the utmost indifference to human suffering. The celebrated novelist Pa Chin (Li Pai Kan) saw Emma Goldman as his 'spiritual mother' and constructed his pseudonym from one syllable each of the names Bakunin and Kropotkin. Needless to say, he was subjected to 're-education' several times, and, in 1989, at the age of 84, was arrested because of his support for the demonstrators in Tiananmen Square.

But the country where anarchism put down its deepest roots was Spain, which in the 1930s had both a mass anarcho-syndicalist trade union, the CNT (*Confederación Nacional del Trabajo*), and the FAI (*Federación Anarquista Iberica*), an anarchist body which emerged periodically from an underground existence. The revolution of 19 July 1936 in Spain illustrates another gulf between the anarchist account of events and the way they are perceived and described by more influential voices.

On 18 July 1936, Spain had three Popular Front governments in the course of a single day, debating how to oppose the military revolt from the generals in Morocco, which was moving into mainland Spain, and usually concluding that resistance was futile. Meanwhile in several cities and regions, not only were the weapons of the military garrisons and the civil guards seized, but CNT members took control of factories, transport, and land. The following day marked the beginning, not only of a war against Franco's insurrection, but of a popular revolution.

Franco's rebellion was aided by weapons, troops, and bomber aircraft from Mussolini's Italy and Nazi Germany, but the Non-Intervention Agreement upheld by the British and French governments limited the supply of arms for the anti-Fascist forces

8. In 1936 the workers of the CNT/FAI took over Barcelona's transport system and improved its services for the people.

to those provided (at the cost of Spain's gold reserves) by the Soviet Union. A futher heavy penalty was paid for Soviet support. Stalin's foreign policy required the repudiation of the Spanish revolution in the interests of the 'Popular Front' concept. In the effort to resist growing Soviet influence, anarchist and syndicalist militants actually became ministers both in the Catalan government in Barcelona and in the central government in Madrid.

The war in Spain wound down to its desolate conclusion in April 1939, after immense loss of life. In August that year the non-aggression pact between Stalin and Hitler was signed, and in September the Second World War began. Franco's regime in Spain survived until the dictator's death in 1975. The collapse of opposition brought a relentless campaign of vengeance against those who dared to oppose Franco. There were untold numbers of executions and the prisons were filled. Millions of Spaniards lived out their lives in exile.

9. **Threshing the corn on a farm in Aragon, taken over by its workers in 1936.**

From the point of view of the anarchists, Spain thus provided terrible ironies. In terms of the collectivization of agriculture and industry, it gave a living and inspiring example of Kropotkin's theories about the seizure of control by the workers. In those parts of the country that had not been seized by army units supporting Franco there were large-scale seizures of land. Spain was a predominantly agricultural country, in which 67% of the land was owned by 2% of landowners. At the same time many smallholdings were too small to feed a family. Gerald Brenan, in his classic book *The Spanish Labyrinth*, explained that 'the only reasonable solution through wide tracts of Spain is a collective one'.

In 1936 it was estimated that in those parts of Spain not overrun by Franco's troops, about three million men, women, and children were living in collectivized communes. Observers from the time similarly reported on the collectivization of factories in Catalonia and of the reorganization of public services, transport, telephones, gas, and electricity in Barcelona.

10. 'The Land is Yours: Work It!', slogan on a train in Catalonia, 1936.

The American philosopher of language Noam Chomsky remembers reading about these achievements as a boy in New York, in the Yiddish-language anarchist journal *Fraye Arbeter Shtime*. There stayed in his mind a report on a poverty-stricken Spanish town, Membrilla, in whose miserable huts eight thousand people lived, with 'no newspaper, no cinema, neither a cafe nor a library'. But the villagers shared food, clothing, and tools, and took in a large number of refugees. 'It was, however, not a socialisation of wealth but of poverty . . . Membrilla is perhaps the poorest village of Spain, but it is the most just.' Chomsky comments that

> An account such as this, with its concern for human relations and the ideal of a just society, must appear very strange to the consciousness of the sophisticated intellectual, and it is therefore treated with scorn, or taken to be naive or primitive or otherwise irrational. Only when such prejudice is abandoned will it be possible for historians to undertake a serious study of the popular movement that transformed Republican Spain in one of the most remarkable social revolutions that history records.

By now the serious studies have been made, and Chomsky has stressed their significance and their lessons for the future, since, as he says,

> What attracts me about anarchism personally are the tendencies in it that try to come to grips with the problems of dealing with complex organised industrial societies within a framework of free institutions and structures.

The Spanish experience hardly met the second of his criteria, but the events of 1936 amply justified his comments. These achievements were barely noticed in the news media of Western Europe outside the journals of anarchism and the non-communist far Left, and when George Orwell, back from Spain, attempted to puncture the conspiracy of silence in his *Homage to Catalonia* in 1937, his book had sold a mere 300 copies before being remaindered to the anarchist bookshop in 1940. Many decades later, Ken Loach's film *Land and Freedom* (1995) was rapturously received in Spain for dramatizing a key episode in the civil war, hitherto almost unknown in Spain itself.

Needless to say, in the years of exile, those anarchists who had survived both the war and Franco's revenge devoted endless debate to the fatal decision of the leaders of the CNT to become part of government in an effort to combat Soviet dominance. Since every variety of anarchism has opposed the structure of politics and the political system, this decision was seen as a compromise that brought no advantage and much discredit. Those anarchists who have explored the issue tend to agree with the comment of the veteran French anarchist Sébastien Faure: 'I am aware of the fact that it is not always possible to do what one should do; but I know that there are things that on no account can one ever do.'

Meanwhile, decades later, a new series of popular uprisings rediscovered anarchist slogans in heroic defiance of Stalin's apparently monolithic empire. Suppressed aspirations emerged on the streets of Hungarian and Polish cities in 1956 and on those of Czechoslovakia in 1968. They were harbingers of the subsequent bloodless collapse of the Soviet Union, after decades of appalling suffering for those who, usually inadvertently, failed to please their rulers.

As the regimes of their jailers collapsed around them, there was some comfort for the surviving anarchists, with their black flags of protest against the new capitalism steered into being by their old oppressors. They were still monotonously right and their priorities remained the same.

Chapter 3
States, societies, and the collapse of socialism

There is a vital distinction, stressed by anarchists, between society and the state. It has been obvious for centuries, and although many political thinkers have ignored this distinction, it was as clear, for example, to such 20th-century academics as Isaiah Berlin or G. D. H. Cole as it was in the 18th century to Thomas Paine, cited in the previous chapter. However, accompanying the collapse of the Soviet Empire there has been a rediscovery by political enquirers of 'civil society'.

The philosopher Martin Buber was the friend and executor of the German anarchist Gustav Landauer, whose observation about the nature of the state as a mode of human behaviour is discussed in Chapter 1. In his capacity as a professor of sociology, Buber provided a striking polarization of the two principles of human behaviour involved: the political and the social. He saw the characteristics of the political principle to be power, authority, hierarchy, and dominion, while the social principle was visible to him in all spontaneous human associations built around a common need or common interest. The problem that arose was that of identifying the reason for the continual ascendancy of the political principle. Buber's answer suggested that

> the fact that every people feels itself threatened by the others gives
> the state its definite unifying power; it depends upon the instinct of

self-preservation of society itself; the latent external crisis enables it to get the upper hand in internal crises . . . All forms of government have this in common: each possesses more power than is required by the given conditions; in fact, this excess in the capacity for making dispositions is actually what we understand by political power. The measure of this excess . . . represents the exact difference between administration and government.

Buber described this excess, which he admitted could not be computed exactly, as the 'political surplus', and observed that

its justification derives from the external and internal instability, from the latent state of crisis between nations and within every nation. The political principle is always stronger in relation to the social principle than the given conditions require. The result is a continuous diminution in social spontaneity.

Social spontaneity is highly valued by anarchists but is not on the agenda of the politicians involved in dismantling the British post-war welfare state, and recommending the virtues of profit-making private enterprise. Anarchists are frequently told that their antipathy to the state is historically outmoded, since a main function of the modern state is the provision of social welfare. They respond by stressing that social welfare in Britain did not originate from government, nor from the post-war National Insurance laws, nor with the initiation of the National Health Service in 1948. It evolved from the vast network of friendly societies and mutual aid organizations that had sprung up through working-class self-help in the 19th century.

The founding father of the NHS was the then member of parliament for Tredegar in South Wales, Aneurin Bevan, the Labour Government's Minister of Health. His constituency was the home of the Tredegar Medical Society, founded in 1870 and surviving until 1995. It provided medical care for the local employed workers, who were mostly miners and steelworkers, but also (unlike the pre-1948

National Health Insurance) for the needs of dependants, children, the old, and the non-employed: everyone living in the district. It was

> sustained through the years by voluntary contributions of three old pennies in the pound from the wage-packets of miners and steelworkers ... At one time the society employed five doctors, a dentist, a chiropodist and a physiotherapist to care for the health of about 25,000 people.

A retired miner told Peter Hennessy that when Bevan initiated the National Health Service, 'We thought he was turning the whole country into one big Tredegar.' In practice, the Health Service has been in a state of continuous reorganization ever since its foundation, but has never been submitted to a local and federalized approach to medical care. A second reflection on the story of Tredegar is that when every employed worker in that town paid a voluntary levy to extend the local medical service to every resident, the earnings of even highly skilled industrial workers were below the liability to income tax. But ever since full employment and the system of PAYE (automatic deduction of tax as a duty of employers) was introduced during the Second World War, the central government's Treasury has creamed off the cash that once supported local initiatives. If the pattern of local self-taxation on the Tredegar model had become the general pattern for health provision, this permanent daily need would not have become the plaything of central government financial policy.

Anarchists cite this little, local example of an alternative approach to the provision of health care to indicate that a different style of social organization could have evolved. In British experience, another variety was to be found in the 1930s and 1950s in what became known as the Peckham Experiment in south London, which was essentially a family health club where medical care was a feature of a social club providing sporting and swimming facilities. These and much more recent attempts to change the relationships in meeting universal social needs exemplify the urgency of the search for alternatives to the dreary polarity of public bureaucracy on the one hand and private profit on the other. I have myself heard the former chief architect to the Ministry of Health admit that the advice he gave for years on hospital design was misguided, and have heard similar confessions from management consultants, expensively hired to solve the NHS's organizational problems.

A century ago, Kropotkin noted the endless variety of 'friendly societies, the unities of oddfellows, the village and town clubs organised for meeting the doctor's bills' built up by working-class self-help; as part of his evidence for *Mutual Aid: A Factor of Evolution*, and in a later book, *Modern Science and Anarchism*, he declared that 'the economic and political liberation of man will have to create new forms for its expression in life, instead of those established by the State'. For he saw it as self-evident that 'this new form will have to be more popular, more decentralised, and nearer to the folk-mote self-government than representative government can ever be'. He reiterated that we will be compelled to find new forms of organization for the social functions that the state fulfils through the bureaucracy, and that 'as long as this is not done, nothing will be done'.

It is often suggested that as a result of modern personal mobility and instant communications, we all live in a series of global villages and that consequently the concept of local control of local services is obsolete. But there is confusion here between the concepts of communities of *propinquity* and communities of *interest*. We may share concerns with people on the other side of the world, and not even *know* our neighbours. But the picture is transformed at different stages in our personal or family history when we have shared interests with other users of the local primary school or health centre, and the local shop or post office. Here there is, as every parent will confirm, an intense concern with very local issues.

Alternative patterns of social control of local facilities *could* have emerged, but for the fact that centralized government imposed national uniformity, while popular disillusionment with the bureaucratic welfare state coincided with the rise of the all-party gospel of managerial capitalism. Anarchists claim that after the inevitable disappointment, an alternative concept of socialism will be rediscovered. They argue that the identification of social welfare with bureaucratic managerialism is one of the factors that has delayed the exploration of other approaches for half a century. The private sector, as it is called, is happy to take over the health needs of those citizens who can pay its bills. Other citizens would either have to suffer the minimal services that remain for them, or to re-create the institutions that they built up in the 19th century. The anarchists see their methods as more relevant than ever, waiting to be reinvented, precisely because modern society has learned the limitations of both socialist and capitalist alternatives.

A once-famous book, James Burnham's *The Managerial Revolution*, traced a shift in power in companies from shareholders to managers. But another more recent change in the power structure of public services of every kind has been felt, for example, all through the education system. It is the rise to dominance of professional managers who are the new unassailable masters of every kind of institution. Middle-class professionals in, say, public health, environmental planning, schools and universities, and the social services have found themselves subjected to the same kind of managerial Newspeak that used to outrage working-class trade unionists. Mastery of its grotesque jargon has become the prerequisite for appointment and promotion throughout the job market, except in the submerged economy of hard repetitive work, where the old assumptions of insecurity, long hours, and low pay remain true.

The new managerialism has such insubstantial foundations and has aroused such resentment among people proud of their professional skills (as was also true of skilled workers displaced by globalization) that it is bound to be challenged by a new breed of advocates of workplace democracy. Already the authors of alternative textbooks of management are borrowing the language, if not the intentions, of the anarchists, for example with a manual entitled *Managing Without Management*, and another called *Action and Existence: Anarchism for Business Administration*.

It seems inevitable that anarchist concepts will be reinvented or rediscovered continually, in fields never envisaged by the propagandists of the past, as people in so many areas of human activity search for alternatives to the crudities and injustices of both free-market capitalism and bureaucratic managerial socialism. It is possible to discern four principles that would shape an anarchist theory of organizations: that they should be (1) voluntary, (2) functional, (3) temporary, and (4) small.

They should be voluntary and functional for obvious reasons. There is no point in advocating individual freedom and responsibility if we go on to set up organizations in which membership is mandatory, or which have no purpose. There is a tendency for bodies to continue to exist after having outlived their functions. They should be temporary precisely because permanence is one of those factors that hardens the arteries of any organization, giving it a vested interest in its own survival, or in serving the interests of its office-holders rather than performing its ostensible functions. Finally, they should be small because in small, face-to-face groups the bureaucratizing and hierarchical tendencies inherent in all organizations have least opportunity to develop.

The 20th century experienced or witnessed every variety of state socialism, and learned that if its rulers are ruthless enough, they can impose, for a while, the most bizarre regimes and describe them as socialism. As socialism has been grossly misrepresented, so anarchism suffers from the widely held view that it is simply another variety of *millenarianism*, the belief in the eventual arrival, 'after the revolution', of a period of ultimate happiness when all the problems that beset humanity will have been solved, permanently.

The 19th-century anarchist propaganda, in common with other varieties of socialist propaganda, frequently implied this, but I have seldom met 20th-century anarchists who admitted to this simple faith. As for the great 20th-century tragedy of the Soviet Union, promising earthly paradise for future generations earned by today's sacrifice, the anarchist inquest on it was written as long ago as 1847 by Bakunin's friend, the Russian populist Alexander Herzen:

> If progress is the goal, for whom then are we working? Who is this Moloch who, as the toilers approach him, instead of rewarding them, draws back, and as a consolation to the exhausted multitudes shouting, 'We, who are about to die, salute thee!', can only give the mocking answer that after their death all will be beautiful on earth. Do you really wish to condemn human beings alive today to the mere sad role of caryatids supporting a floor for others one day to dance upon? Of wretched galley slaves who, up to their knees in mud, drag a barge with the humble words 'Future Progress' on its flag?
>
> A goal which is infinitely remote is not a goal at all, it is a deception. A goal must be closer – at the very least the labourer's wage or pleasure in the work performed. Each epoch, each generation, each life has had, and has, its own experience, and *en route* new demands grow, new methods.

Socialism in the 20th century promised 'jam tomorrow' so regularly, and the promise remained so often unfulfilled, that as Herzen insisted, new generations will have to evolve their own more immediate social aims, which, the anarchists hope, will be structured around styles of social organization other than the machinery of the state.

But because it is frequently suggested that anarchism is simply inappropriate for the *scale* of modern society, the concept of federalism is vital for any attempt to build an anarchist theory of organization. Anarchist approaches to federalism are fully discussed in Chapter 9.

Chapter 4
Deflating nationalism and fundamentalism

The anarchists claim that popular self-organization could provide those new forms of social organization which, as Kropotkin put it in an observation I have cited earlier, would undertake 'those social functions that the state fulfils through the bureaucracy'. However, these are not the only issues that are raised when sceptics dismiss anarchism as a primitive ideology that is simply not relevant to the modern world. They have a different reason, as they observe the modern nation state and the intense hostilities and rivalries arising between the government of any major state and others. Or, indeed, the lethal hatreds visible among different factions within one territory that has been designated as a state, and the frightening antagonisms that emerge between the adherents of different religions. They may notice especially the poisonous legacy of European imperialism to the territories that the empire-building powers seized and colonized.

It is probably still important to remind the British, French, Belgians, Germans, Spanish, Portuguese, Italians, Dutch, Austrians, Greeks, Turks, Russians, and Americans, among others, that most of the intractable disputes around the globe today are a direct result of the imperialist policies of their one-time rulers, with their fatal fascination for seizing some other part of the world, and their cynical application of the slogan 'Divide and Rule'. All around the world people are suffering today as a result of the activity of the empire-builders, and militant attitudes usually succeed in making matters worse. For nationalist movements, as Avi Shlaim has expressed it,

> have an in-built tendency towards extremism and xenophobia, towards self-righteousness on the one hand and demonising the enemy on the other. History is often falsified and even fabricated to serve a nationalist political agenda.

It is hard to see how the anarchists, with an absolute hostility to both religious rivalries and territorial politics, can engage in these disputes, beyond the direct rejection of imperialism, except to wish that they were in the past. Abstention itself can be a perilous, though necessary, attitude, and we have all observed around the globe instances when the zealots have turned their most vicious attention to those who dare to attempt an accommodation with the people on 'the other side'. Martin Buber, who, half a century ago, made some valuable contributions to an assessment of anarchism, warned his fellow Zionists as long ago as 1921 that if the Jews in Palestine did not live *with* the Arabs as well as *next* to them, they would find themselves living in enmity with them. When he died, 44 years later, the obituarists noted that his advocacy of bi-nationalism caused him to be ostracized by the orthodox as 'an enemy of the people'.

These 20th-century responses were certainly not anticipated by the 19th-century anarchists. Their classical statement on religion as a social phenomenon came from the most widely circulated work of the Russian anarchist Michael Bakunin, *God and the State*. In this fragment, written in 1871, he deplores the fact that belief in God still survived among the people, especially, as he put it, 'in the rural districts, where it is more widespread than among the proletariat of the cities'. He thought this faith in religion was all too natural, since all governments profited from the ignorance of the people as one of the essential conditions of their own power; while weighed down by labour, deprived of leisure and of intellectual intercourse, the people sought an escape. Bakunin claimed that there were three routes of escape from the miseries of life, two of them illusory and one real. The first two were the bottle and the church, 'debauchery of the body or debauchery of the mind; the third is social revolution'. Social revolution, he asserted,

> will be much more potent than all the theological propagandism of the freethinkers to destroy to their last vestige the religious beliefs and dissolute habits of the people, beliefs and habits much more intimately connected than is generally supposed.

Bakunin then turned to the powerful, dominant classes in society who, while too worldly-wise to be believers themselves, 'must at least make a semblance of believing' because the simple faith of the people was a useful factor in keeping them down. Finally, in this particular statement of his attitudes, Bakunin turns to those propagandists for religion who, when you challenge them on any specific absurdity in their dogma, relating to miracles, virgin births, or resurrection, loftily explain that they are to be understood as beautiful myths rather than literal truths, and that *we* are to be pitied for our prosaic questions, rather than *them* for propagating mythology as truth.

Bakunin's opinions were much the same on this matter as those of his adversary Karl Marx, one of whose best-known phrases was his description of religion as the 'opium of the people'. And the historians of ideas would categorize liberalism, socialism, communism, and anarchism all as products of the period known as the Enlightenment, the result of the Age of Reason, the ferment of ideas and the spirit of enquiry between the English Revolution of the 1640s and the American and French revolutions of the 1770s and 1780s.

In parochial English terms, one slow, grudgingly conceded result of the Enlightenment was religious toleration. We tend to forget that

England has a state church, founded because of a row that Henry VIII had with the Pope over one of his divorces. It too claimed its martyrs, as the long history of the suppression of dissenters reminds us, as does the continual struggle for religious freedom. It wasn't until 1858 that legal disabilities were lifted from believing Jews, and not until 1871 that people who could not subscribe to the 39 Articles of the Church of England were admitted to the ancient universities. The Church of England may be an irrelevance to the majority of the British people, but it is a reminder of an important social and political fact. One result of the Enlightenment was that the people who wrote the constitutions of many states sought to learn the lessons of history and the horrors of religious wars by insisting on the absolute separation of religious practices from *public* life. Religion was to be a private affair.

This was true of the founding fathers of the United States of America, whose ancestors had fled religious persecution in Europe; it was true of the French Republic, and consequently of those countries which, with immense loss of life, liberated themselves from French imperialism. And it is true of many new republics similarly founded as a result of the collapse of imperialism in the 20th century. Some key examples are the republics of India, Turkey, Egypt, Algeria, and Israel.

Now, all over the world, the secular state is under threat. Secular political regimes in North Africa and the Middle East are confronted by militant religious movements, and there is a growing fundamentalist threat to the secular constitution of the United States. This isn't what Bakunin or Marx, or any other political thinker of the 19th century, from Alexis de Tocqueville to John Stuart Mill, predicted.

The unexpected and unwelcome change in the religious atmosphere which we call fundamentalism arose from a trend in religious revivalism in the United States after the First World War, which insisted on belief in the literal truth of everything in the Bible. The use of the term has spread to describe trends in the Jewish, Muslim, Hindu, Sikh, and Shinto religions which, to outsiders, present similar features. They are a threat not only to the hard-won concept of the secular state, which anarchists may not feel to be important, but to the hard-won freedoms of every citizen. The anarchist and secularist propagandist Nicolas Walter urged us to take this threat seriously, stressing that

> Fundamentalist Christians are trying to suppress the study of evolution and the practice of contraception and abortion in the West and the Third World. Fundamentalist Jews are trying to incorpoate the whole of Palestine into Israel and to impose the *halachah*, the traditional law of Judaism. Fundamentalist Muslims are trying to establish Muslim regimes in all countries with Muslim populations (including Britain) and to impose the *sharia*, the traditional law of Islam. And fundamentalists of all faiths are using assassination and terror all over the world to suppress freedom and discussion of such matters.

This is an absolute tragedy for that majority of citizens in any country who are simply concerned with the ordinary business of living, feeding a family, and enjoying the daily pleasures of life, as well as for those who aspire to improve conditions through community action and social justice.

Governmental suppression of religion never works. The Soviet Union witnessed 70 years of state hostility, sometimes violent and sometimes benign, to religious activity. When the regime collapsed, there was a huge revival of the Orthodox faith and a happy hunting ground for American Protestant evangelists. In Soviet Central Asia, Malise Ruthven suggests,

> the local elites, attached to Islamic customs and recognising a degree of affinity between Islamic and social values, cheated on their anti-religious activities as assiduously as they faked their

cotton-production figures. Gatherings of old men reading the Koran would be described to zealots of the Society for Scientific Atheism as meetings of Great Patriotic War veterans.

In Turkey, Kemal Ataturk, who also shared Bakunin's views on religion, embarked on a dictatorial policy of what we might call 'de-Islamification'. His current successors are prevented from instituting even a façade of democracy precisely because of the threat of the return of religion. On a different time-scale, the Shah of Iran, who was a ruthless Westernizer, was succeeded by a fundamentalist regime that no one predicted. Egypt and Algeria are torn apart by rival elites of the secular or religious state. In the United States the most powerful of all political lobbies is that of the Christian Coalition, with a growing influence in the Republican Party. It denies any responsibility for the murder of the last doctor to perform an abortion in the American South.

It is disappointing and unexpected for secularist anarchists, who thought that wars of religion belonged to the past, now to have to confront issues of the recognition of difference, while they are trying to move on to the issues that unite rather than divide us. One approach they can take is that of the anarchist propagandist Rudolf Rocker, a century ago, in the Jewish community of Whitechapel in east London. Some secularist allies had chosen the propaganda of provocative behaviour on Sabbath mornings outside the synagogue in Brick Lane. Asked his opinion of these demonstrations, Rocker replied that the place for believers was the house of worship, and the place for non-believers was the radical meeting. But the scene has changed. For the same building that has seen many faiths come and go, as a Huguenot church, a dissenting meeting-house, and a Jewish synagogue, is now a mosque. Anyone harassing the emerging worshippers today is not a secularist Bangladeshi but an English racist, menacing and heavy, bent on instilling fear and making trouble.

It has been said, for example, of the Bharatiya Janata ('Indian People's') Party (BJP) in India, who succeeded in spreading communal violence into parts of the Punjab where different communities had previously lived in harmony together, that the name of the disease is not fundamentalism but ethnic nationalism. This view fits other parts of the globe, and in such instances, including many areas of the Islamic world, we can again choose to blame the endless humiliations and devaluations of the local culture inflicted by Western imperialism.

Edward Said's difficult diagnosis (see box below) envelops big truths. The countries of the Near and Middle East were for

> **The fear and terror induced by the overscale images of 'terrorism' and 'fundamentalism' – call them the figures of an international or transnational imagery made up of foreign devils – hastens the individual's subordination to the dominant norms of the moment. This is as true in the new post-colonial societies as it is in the West generally and the United States particularly. Thus to oppose the abnormality and extremism embedded in terrorism and fundamentalism – my example has only a small degree of parody – is also to uphold the moderation, rationality, executive centrality of a vaguely designated 'Western' (or otherwise local and patriotically assumed) ethos. The irony is that far from endowing the Western ethos with the confidence and secure 'normality' we associate with privilege and rectitude, this dynamic imbues 'us' with a righteous anger and defensiveness in which 'others' are finally seen as enemies, bent on destroying our civilisation and way of life.**
>
> Edward W. Said, *Culture and Imperialism*
>
> (London: Chatto and Windus, 1993)

centuries subjected to one imperialism or another, their cultures ridiculed or patronized, and even their boundaries formed by lines drawn on the map by European governments and business. They are valued today according to their oil resources or as potential markets, while they are awash with weapons left over from Cold War bribes. The Western secular religion of conspicuous consumption was readily adopted by Middle Eastern rulers, but they offered nothing but frustrated hopes to the poor majority of their subjects.

Another vital issue was raised by the Moroccan scholar Fatima Mernissi, when she was asked to provide a preface for the English translation of her book on *Women and Islam*.

> When I finished writing this book I had come to understand one thing: if women's rights are a problem for some modern Muslim men, it is neither because of the Koran, nor the Prophet, nor the Islamic tradition, but simply because those rights conflict with the interests of a male elite. The elite faction is trying to convince us that their egotistical, highly subjective and mediocre view of culture and society has a sacred basis.

In common with all the other left-wing factions of the late 19th and early 20th centuries, the anarchists saw territorial and religious separatism as irrelevant preoccupations that human society had outgrown. Their only possible message is the hope that zealotry will lose its impetus when its leaders find they have no followers, as people discover more interesting, more enjoyable, or at the very least less lethal, issues to discuss with their neighbours.

Chapter 5
Containing deviancy and liberating work

From the fall of the Bastille in 1789, which actually released only seven prisoners, to the death of Stalin in 1953, which slowly liberated millions, the anarchists, through personal experience, provided an impressive literature on the defects of the penal system. Kropotkin's first book was his account of his experiences *In Russian and French Prisons* (1887), and Alexander Berkman's was his *Prison Memoirs of an Anarchist* (1912).

It was Kropotkin who first used the phrase 'prisons are the universities of crime', and his observation remains true in the sense that the first imprisonment of any offender becomes a guarantee that he, like the people with whom he shares a cell, will learn in jail a long series of more sophisticated criminal techniques than the petty larceny that started off his prison career. Kropotkin claimed in 1886 that a society built around cooperation rather than competition would, for that very reason, suffer less from antisocial activity. He argued that

> Peoples without political organisation, and therefore less depraved
> than ourselves, have perfectly understood that the man who is called
> 'criminal' is simply unfortunate; that the remedy is not to flog him,
> to chain him up, or to kill him on the scaffold or in prison, but to
> help him by the most brotherly care, by treatment based on equality,
> by the usages of life amongst honest men.

It could be claimed that the best service the British and American governments in the two world wars of the 20th century could have provided to the cause of penal reform was the imprisonment of war-resisters. The jailed objectors, beyond the appalling hardships that befell some of them in the First World War, had several important attributes. They tended to be literate people and keen observers of their surroundings and of their fellow prisoners. They also had a useful sense of moral superiority over their jailers, seeing the humiliations they suffered as a reflection, not of their own situation, but of that of the good citizens who had chosen to incarcerate them.

These observers recognized and publicized what a handful of 19th-century reformers had already pointed out: that many of their fellow prisoners, serving the current prison sentence for a lifetime career of petty theft, petty violence, drug-dealing, or drunken idiocy, came from a background that made their offences and incarceration almost inevitable. Many of us, learning the cost to the citizen of keeping any individual in jail, and realizing that it is far more than our own incomes, could fervently wish that we had taken heed of the warnings of the penal reformers, who had sought to draw our attention to the common factors in the lives of the people we imprison. Frequently, for example, inmates have a background of institutional childhood, of mental instability, or of educational failure. They are also, overwhelmingly, male.

Recognition of these factors was one of the influences at the end of the 19th century leading to the establishment in both Britain and America of the probation service, in which, as an alternative to prison, a probation officer was charged with the task of becoming the friend and advisor of the offender, and with helping him to lead a normal working and family life. Through much of the 20th century there was a slow humanization of the penal system, so far as this was possible, inspired by the reformers who had been inmates and observers in the war years, despite frequent opposition from the staff of penal establishments.

Practitioners of various therapeutic approaches gained access, sporadically, to the penal system, with the support of some prison governors, with significant results. They urged the prison staff that their own status and job satisfaction would be enhanced if their work was perceived as curative rather than custodial. Many anarchists were sceptical about these efforts to civilize the penal system, and so, of course, was the popular press, which regularly described open prisons as holiday camps (revealing their journalists' ignorance of both). In the decades following the Second World War, many countries witnessed a steady decline in the prison population. (Notable exceptions were the Soviet Union and the nations whose governments it influenced.) David Cayley explained that

> The Netherlands set the standard, bringing a rate of 90 prisoners per 100,000 of population after the war down to a remarkable 17 per 100,000 in 1975 ... Reductions in imprisonment had been brought about by what Dutch criminologist Willem de Haan once called the 'politics of bad conscience.'

But from the late 1970s onwards, the politics of bad conscience were replaced by the contrasting approach described by the criminologist Andrew Rutherford as 'a politics of good conscience about imprisonment'. Criminal statistics are notoriously difficult to interpret, because they reflect simply the number of arrests for a range of offences that any police force is expected to record. But penal statistics are readily available and tell a terrifying story. David Cayley reported in 1998 that

> To help house the 1.5 million Americans currently in prison, 168 new state prisons and 45 new federal prisons were built between 1990 and 1995 alone, but these were still not enough to accommodate the numbers of new prisoners ... The United States

has now exposed so many of its citizens – especially its Black and Hispanic citizens – to the brutalizing effects of its prisons that a self-fulfilling prophecy has been set in motion. The more Americans who are manhandled by the criminal justice system, the more there are whose behaviour seems to justify and demand this treatment.

By the year 2000, prisons in the United States had received their two-millionth inmate. The sociologist David Downes remarked at a conference on crime at New York University that no other nation in history has ever put a bigger proportion of its citizens in jail. The judicial system also ensures that African-American men have a 1 in 4 chance of going to prison during their lifetimes, while the chance is 1 in 23 for their white fellow citizens. Professor Downes was asked whether Europe would be affected by the American example. He replied that 'The components of a steep rise in imprisonment in Europe have already been assembled.' His answer was correct, and Britain leads Europe in the proportion of its citizens that it incarcerates. Alternative approaches, shared by the anarchists with other penal reformers, have been rejected by the politicians and their public. This does not persuade reformers to change their opinions, but merely to await an eventual shift in public attitudes.

There is just one field of law-breaking and law-enforcement in which a policy of *decriminalization* is gaining advocates, and which would greatly reduce the prison population. This concerns the imprisonment of drug users and drug traders. Everyone agrees this policy is an expensive failure that, as David Cayley observes, 'has fostered evils far worse than those it was supposed to eliminate'. It has the additional irony that many users find the drugs of their choice are more easily available inside prison than on the outside. Here it is worth noting the opinions of the anarchist Errico Malatesta, as far back as 1922, long before our parents or grandparents imagined that we had a drug problem.

It is the old mistake of legislators, in spite of experience invariably showing that laws, however barbarous they may be, have never served to suppress vice or to discourage delinquency. The more severe the penalties imposed on the consumers and traffickers of cocaine, the greater will be the attractions of forbidden fruits and the fascination of the risks incurred by the consumer, and the greater will be the profits made by the speculators, avid for money.

It is useless, therefore, to hope for anything from the law. We must suggest another solution. Make the use and sale of cocaine free from restrictions, and open kiosks where it would be sold at cost price or even under cost. And *then* launch a great propaganda campaign to explain to the public, and let them see for themselves, the evils of cocaine; no one would engage in counter-propaganda because no one could exploit the misfortune of addicts.

Certainly the harmful use of cocaine would not disappear completely, because the social causes which create and drive those poor devils to the use of drugs would still exist. But in any case the evil would decrease, because nobody could make profits out of its sale, and nobody could speculate on the hunt for speculators. And for this reason our suggestion either will not be taken into account, or it will be considered impractical and mad. Yet intelligent and disinterested people might say to themselves: Since the penal laws have proved to be impotent, would it not be a good thing, as an experiment, to try out the anarchist method?

Errico Malatesta in *Umanità Nova*, 2 September 1920,
reprinted in V. Richards (ed.), *Errico Malatesta: His Life and Ideas*
(London: Freedom Press, 1965)

In two European cities, Zurich and Amsterdam, local authorities have boldly sought to implement such a policy, and in Britain, by the beginning of the 21st century, at least two chief constables have expressed a similar point of view, earning sensational headlines but little practical support.

Politicians of the major parties in Britain won popular acclaim with rhetoric about giving offenders a 'short, sharp shock' or sending them to 'Boot Camps', and by circumscribing the efforts of the probation service to keep released offenders out of jail. Even the staccato, single-syllable language of these programmes indicates that the intention was not to cope with the problem of crime but to satisfy the headline-writers of the popular press, the real determinants of penal policy. In the United States, the Republican Party's electoral success is seen to be related to its ability to portray its opponents as 'soft on crime'.

Meanwhile, suicides grew among young prisoners jailed for offences that were a nuisance, rather than a threat, to society. Moreover, it is perfectly obvious that prison does nothing to reduce the crime rate. As Lord Waddington, Home Secretary to Margaret Thatcher, put it, 'Prison is a very expensive way of making bad men worse'. Even the politicians no longer believe in the policies they administer. This is hardly surprising when you consider the statistics. In 2003 it was reported that 84% of young people released from custodial sentences in Britain rapidly reoffend. Figures from the United States would exceed this record.

But the issues raised by the anarchists, among the ranks of the penal reformers, will not disappear. They are made more intractable by society's assumptions, as manipulated by the popular press.

Another crucial question, which arose early in the history of anarchism, concerned its application to the world of work, especially since the anarchist pioneers tended to have links with the emerging trade union movement. They identified with the radical end of the union spectrum, proclaiming anarcho-syndicalism (from the French *syndicat*, meaning union), which saw every local industrial struggle as a step towards a general strike, when the collapse of capitalism would lead to a take-over by the workers.

In France the *Confédération Générale du Travail* (CGT) and in Spain the *Confederación Nacional del Trabajo* (CNT) became large-scale mass movements, as, for a time, did the Industrial Workers of the World (IWW) in the United States. There were, of course, inbuilt conflicts within syndicalist unions, between those members who were willing to fight and sometimes win little local battles over small issues, and the militants who hoped to turn every small dispute into the final struggle to seize control of the means of production and thus 'expropriate the expropriators', continuing production under workers' control.

But the fading away of the aim of liberating work has little to do with the gulf between reformers and revolutionaries in the workers' organizations. It has a far closer connection with the new, ultimate weapon in the hands of employers against the claims of workers: 'accept our conditions or we will transfer our activities and your jobs to South-east Asia or Latin America, where the labour force will be delighted to work on our terms.' The owners of capital remain in the rich world, but the providers of labour are now in the developing world, and if they should demand a larger share of the products of their work, the employers simply shift to a cheaper labour force in another country.

Meanwhile, the rich world has a concealed labour force of its own. Agricultural work in the picking and packing of fruit and vegetables is undertaken by gang-masters with their teams of illegal immigrants, East European public employees waiting for wages in their own countries, students, and migrants. Another underclass copes with telephone and Internet enquiries, operating in call centres from provincial Britain to Bangalore in India.

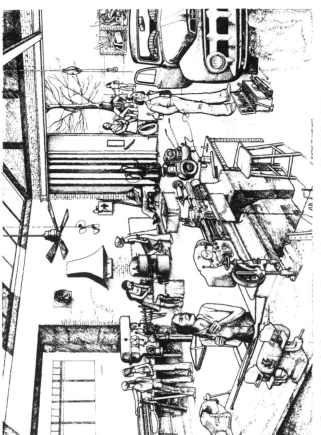

11. Liberating work: the community workshop, as envisaged by Clifford Harper.

A century ago, the 'new unionism' in Britain and the IWW in America set about organizing and representing the unskilled and uncounted workers on the fringes of the official economy, and succeeded. At the same time, the anarchist Kropotkin was addressing a British audience which assumed that Britain was the workshop of the world, and that for ever more the whole globe would depend on textiles from Lancashire, coal from Newcastle, and ships from the Clyde. In 1899, when he wrote his *Fields, Factories and Workshops*, one of his aims was to demonstrate that, while the politicians and economists thought in terms of vast factories, the greater part of industrial production was actually carried out in small workshops and little local enterprises. Electricity and modern transport had decentralized production, and Kropotkin urged that this liberated not only the location of work but the individual's choice of occupation. It was now possible to combine brain work and manual work, which was his industrial ideal.

Anarchists are seldom to be found in the diminishing world of career employment in formal industry or bureaucracy. They tend to find their niche in the informal or small-scale economy. This is not surprising, since industrial psychologists frequently report that satisfaction in work is directly related to the 'span of autonomy' it offers, meaning the amount of the working day or week in which the workers are free to make their own decisions. In this post-industrial world of work, the only serious study of the small businessman finds him to be not a Thatcherite hero, but a creative rebel against the compulsion to be either an employer or an employee. Paul Thompson reports that

> It turns out that far from being an especially purposeful breed of men, Samuel Smiles' heroes a hundred years on, many small businessmen are closer to a kind of drop-out. They disliked the whole modern capitalist ethic, and especially being employed by others; instead they preferred to feel the satisfaction of providing a 'service' and 'doing a good job'. Quite often it was a mere chance that

allowed them to find their present vocation. Moreover, they will not provide the basis for our next industrial revolution, because they don't want to expand: that would imply employing people and losing the personal relationships they like to have with a small number of workers.

Findings like these are far from the expectations of the anarcho-syndicalists, who envisaged a triumphant take-over of the factory by its workers, but they indicate clearly that anarchist aspirations are close to the dreams of vast numbers of citizens who feel trapped by the culture of employment.

Chapter 6
Freedom in education

The editors of a well-known anthology of anarchist writings remark that, from the school prospectus issued by William Godwin in 1783 to Paul Goodman's book of 1964 on *Compulsory Miseducation*, 'no other movement whatever has assigned to educational principles, concepts, experiments and practices a more significant place in its writings and activities'. Godwin's tract was published as *An Account of the Seminary that will be Opened on Monday the Fourth Day of August, at Epsom in Surrey, for the Instruction of Twelve Pupils*. It failed to convince enough parents, and the school never opened. In this pamphlet he declared that

> modern education not only corrupts the heart of our youth, by the rigid slavery to which it condemns them, it also undermines their reason, by the unintelligible jargon with which they are overwhelmed in the first instance, and the little attention that is given to accommodating their pursuits to their capacities in the second.

And he added that

> there is not in the world a truer object of pity than a child terrified at every glance, and watching with anxious uncertainty the caprices of a pedagogue.

A later book of Godwin's, *The Enquirer* (1797), contains, as
his biographer rightly says, 'some of the most remarkable and
advanced ideas on education ever written'. Its opening words are
the splendid affirmation that 'The true object of education, like
that of every other moral process, is the generation of happiness'.
And it goes on to assert the rights of the child against the automatic
assumptions of authority by the adult world. For example, he
observed that

> Children, it is said, are free from the cares of the world. Are they
> without their cares? Of all cares, those that bring with them the
> greatest consolation are the cares of independence. There is no more
> certain source of exultation than the consciousness that I am of
> some importance in the world. A child usually feels that he is a
> nobody. Parents, in the abundance of their providence, take good
> care to administer to them this bitter recollection. How suddenly
> does a child rise to an enviable degree of happiness, who feels that
> he has the honour to be trusted and consulted by his superiors?

Between these two resounding manifestos came Godwin's
best-known book, his *Enquiry Concerning Political Justice* (1793).
In the course of this book he diverged sharply from progressive
opinion in Britain and from the Enlightenment philosophers
Rousseau, Helvetius, Diderot, and Condorcet, all of whom put
forward schemes for national systems of schooling, postulating an
ideal state, which in Godwin's view was a contradiction in terms.
He outlined his three major objections thus:

> The injuries that result from a system of national education are, in
> the first place, that all public establishments include in them the
> idea of permanence ... public education has always expended its
> energies in the support of prejudice ... This feature runs through
> every species of public establishment; and even in the petty
> institution of Sunday schools, the chief lessons to be taught are a
> superstitious veneration for the Church of England, and to bow to
> every man in a handsome coat ...

Secondly, the idea of national education is founded in an inattention to the nature of mind. Whatever each man does for himself is done well; whatever his neighbours or his country undertake to do for him is done ill. It is our wisdom to incite men to act for themselves, not to retain them in a state of perpetual pupillage . . .

Thirdly, the project of a national education ought uniformly to be discouraged on account of its obvious alliance with national government. This is an alliance of a more formidable nature than the old and much contested alliance of church and state. Before we put so powerful a machine under the direction of so ambitious an agent, it behoves us to consider well what we do. Government will not fail to employ it to strengthen its hand and perpetuate its institutions . . . Their views as instigators of a system of education will not fail to be analogous to their views in their political capacity . . . [Even] in the countries where liberty chiefly prevails, it is reasonably to be assumed that there are important errors, and a national system has the most direct tendency to perpetuate those errors and to form all minds on one model.

Some admirers of Godwin's thought have been embarrassed by this rejection of 'progressive' opinion. They recall the hard struggle to achieve free, universal, compulsory education for all in both Britain and the United States after 1870. (There is a confusing similarity of educational language in Britain and the United States. In the United States 'public' schools are the primary and secondary schools provided at the public expense. In Britain 'private' and 'public' are the words used to describe the junior and senior schools funded by affluent parents for their privileged children; the schools described as 'state' schools are actually administered by local government authorities.) In Britain, a centenary publication from the National Union of Teachers in 1970 explained that 'apart from religious and charitable schools, "dame" or common schools were operated by the private enterprise of people who were often barely literate', and it dismissed the widespread working-class hostility to the School Boards of the 19th century with the remark that 'parents were not always quick to appreciate the advantages of full-time schooling against the loss of extra wages'.

But more recently historians have seen this resistance to state schooling in a quite different light. Stephen Humphries found that, by the 1860s, working-class private schools (as opposed to what is meant today by private schools) were providing an alternative education to that of the charitable or religious 'National' or 'British' schools for about one-third of all working-class children, and he suggests that

> This enormous demand for private as opposed to public education is perhaps best illustrated by the fact that working-class parents in a number of major cities responded to the introduction of compulsory attendance regulations not by sending their children to provided state schools, as government inspectors had predicted, but by extending the length of their children's education in private schools. Parents favoured these schools for a number of reasons: they were small and close to home and were consequently more personal and more convenient than most publicly provided schools; they were informal and tolerant of irregular attendance and unpunctuality; no attendance registers were kept; they were not segregated according to age and sex; they used individual as opposed to authoritarian teaching methods; and, most important, they belonged to and were controlled by the local community rather than being imposed on the neighbourhood by an alien authority.

Humphries' remarkable observation was reinforced by a mass of contemporary evidence exhumed by Philip Gardner in his book on *The Lost Elementary Schools of Victorian England*. This researcher concluded that these working-class schools

> achieved just what the customer wanted: quick results in basic skills like reading, writing and arithmetic, wasted no time on religious studies and moral uplift, and represented a genuinely alternative

approach to childhood learning to that prescribed by the education experts.

In the view of the historian Paul Thompson, the price of eliminating these schools through the imposition of the national education system was

> the suppression in countless working-class children of the appetite for education and ability to learn independently which contemporary progressive education seeks to rekindle.

Radically different as it is from the history of education as taught to student teachers, this approach helps us to locate the anarchist thinkers in the spectrum of educational ideas. These include, for example, the speculations of Leo Tolstoy on the school he started at Yasnaya Polyana, and those of Francesco Ferrer (1859–1909), the founder of the 'Modern School' movement. Ferrer opened his first school in Barcelona in 1901, aiming at a secular, rationalist education. He inspired emulators in several countries and aroused the enmity of the church. When the Spanish government called for conscription in Catalonia for its war in Morocco in 1909, Ferrer was held responsible for street battles in Barcelona in which 200 demonstrators were killed, even though he was not present. He was executed, but his campaign for secular education did not die. After the revolution of 19 July 1936, at least 60,000 children in Catalonia attended Ferrer schools.

It is interesting to see how their approach led a variety of anarchists to offer educational opinions in anticipation of the progressive propagandists of a century later. For example, Bakunin, in a mere footnote to a polemic on a different topic, envisaged the school as a lifelong resource for us all:

> They will be schools no longer; they will be popular academies, in which neither pupils nor masters will be known, where the people will come freely to get, if they need it, free instruction, and in which,

12. Mealtime at a Ferrer school in Catalonia. After the revolution of 1936, at least 60,000 children attended Ferrer schools.

rich in their own experience, they will teach in turn many things to the professors who shall bring them knowledge which they lack. This then will be a mutual instruction, an act of intellectual fraternity.

He was writing in 1870, and if his argument is familiar this is precisely because identical aspirations were expressed a century later by people like Ivan Illich and Paul Goodman in America, or in Britain by Michael Young, and by Professor Harry Rée. In 1972 Rée told an audience of young teachers that

I think we are going to see in your lifetime the end of schools as we know them. Instead there will be a community centre with the doors open twelve hours a day, seven days a week, where anybody can wander in and out of the library, workshops, sports centre, self-service store and bar. In a hundred years time the compulsory attendance laws for children to go to school may have gone the same way as the compulsory laws for attendance at church.

His prophecy is unlikely to be fulfilled, for within ten years of his address, an incoming government was blaming the collapse of the British manufacturing industry on, of all unlikely scapegoats, the schools. There followed a new regime of unprecedented intervention by central government in the management and curriculum of primary and secondary schools, which in Britain are provided by local authorities. These included the imposition, for the first time, of a National Curriculum by the central government, a continuous programme of testing children at particular ages, and an avalanche of form-filling for teachers. (This endless assessment proved beyond doubt that schools in affluent districts achieve higher marks than schools in poor areas with a majority of children whose native language is not English. These are social facts that most people already knew.)

By 1995, Her Majesty's Chief Inspector of Schools was declaring that the real impediment to the development of a better educational system in Britain was 'a commitment to particular beliefs about the purposes and conduct of education', and that what was needed was 'less learning by doing and more teaching by telling'. He was repudiating a hundred years of progressive influence on the official, compulsory education system, fitfully moving up the age-range from the nursery to the secondary school. One irony about the rejection of 'progressive' education by politicians of the political Right is that the educational aims of many anarchists would be completely acceptable to them. Michael Smith, the historian of *The Libertarians and Education*, remarks that Proudhon

> was always conscious of the fact that the children he was talking about were the children of workers. Work was going to be their life when they grew up. Proudhon saw nothing wrong with this. The work a man did was something to be proud of, it was what gave interest, value and dignity to his life. It was right, therefore, that school should prepare the young for a life of work. An education that was divorced from the world of work, that is, an education that was entirely bookish or grammar-schoolish in conception, was valueless from the point of view of ordinary working-class children. Of course, an education that went too far in the other direction, which brought up children merely to be fodder for factories, was equally unacceptable. What was required was an education which would equip a child for the workplace but would also give him a degree of independence in the labour market. This could be achieved by giving him not just the basis of a trade but, as well, a whole range of marketable skills which would ensure that he was not totally at the mercy of an industrial system which required specialisation of its workers and then discarded them when the specialisation was no longer of interest to the firm. Thus Proudhon was led to the idea of an education that was 'polytechnical'.

Readers will have guessed, correctly, that Proudhon was concerning himself solely with the education of boys, but this was not true of such successors as Kropotkin, with his hopes for the integration of brain work and manual work, not only in education but in life; nor of such heroes as Francesco Ferrer in Spain, whose approach was similarly that of an education for *emancipation*, as opposed to what he saw as education for *subservience*. Michael Smith's most interesting pages for the English reader describe 'Integral Education' in practice, through the experience of the French anarchist Paul Robin and the school he ran from 1880 to 1894 at Cempius. It was based upon workshop training and the abandonment of the classroom in favour of what we would now call the resource centre. Cooking, needlecraft, carpentry, and metalwork were undertaken by both sexes, while 'the Cempius children, both girls and boys, were among the first children in France to go in for cycling'.

Co-education, sexual equality, and atheism brought down Robin's school, but another celebrated French anarchist, Sébastien Faure, ran a famous school called *La Ruche* ('The Beehive'). Michael Smith comments that 'Faure had learned one very significant lesson from Robin's downfall: stay completely out of the state system and thus be assured of complete independence.' But in Britain there has been a continual effort to introduce the approaches of libertarian education into the school system funded by all citizens. Another historian, John Shotton, has traced the history of these attempts, and of similar efforts to help all those children who have been excluded by the official system.

A century of progressive experiments have had a profound effect on every school, most evidently the primary schools. The role of the teacher has changed from that of fearsome martinet to that of friendly guide, while corporal punishment, once the mainstay of the school system, has been legally outlawed. There is, however, a distinction to be made between 'progressive' education and 'libertarian' education, which in practice revolves around the issue of compulsory or voluntary attendance at lessons. Foremost among the libertarians was A. S. Neill, who for many decades ran Summerhill School in Suffolk, which survives to this day, led by his daughter Zoë Readhead.

13. Beacon Hill School, run by Dora Russell from 1927 to 1943.

Neill could not stand the high-minded and manipulative progressives. By the 1930s he was writing to Dora Russell of Beacon Hill School that she and he were 'the only educators'. As one of his mentors, Homer Lane, put it:

> 'Give the child freedom' is the insistent cry of the New Educators, but then its exponents usually devise a 'system' which, although based on the soundest of principles, limits that freedom and contradicts the principle.

Lane was echoing the opinion of William Godwin in *The Enquirer*, when he found that Rousseau, even though the world was indebted to him 'for the irresistible energy of his writings and the magnitude of his speculations', had fallen into the common error of manipulating the child:

> His whole system of education is a series of tricks, a puppet-show exhibition, of which the master holds the wires, and the scholar is never to suspect in what manner they are moved.

The anarchist approach has been more influential in education than in most other fields of life. It may be contested and deplored by authoritarians, with their own nostalgia for an idealized past, but it is difficult to conceive that young people will tolerate in the future the educational regime to which the grandparents of their rulers were subjected.

In some parts of the world, the battle for the freedom of the young is in the past. In others, it has still to be won. Some of the attempts in Britain to provide an alternative experience for the young people who are excluded from the official education system are described in Chapter 8.

Chapter 7
The individualist response

For a century, anarchists have used the word 'libertarian' as a synonym for 'anarchist', both as a noun and an adjective. The celebrated anarchist journal *Le Libertaire* was founded in 1895. However, much more recently the word has been appropriated by various American free-market philosophers – David Friedman, Robert Nozick, Murray Rothbard, and Robert Paul Wolff – so it is necessary to examine the modern individualist 'libertarian' response from the standpoint of the anarchist tradition.

In approaching this theme, one obstacle to circumnavigate is the German advocate of 'conscious egoism', Max Stirner. He was born Johann Caspar Schmidt (1806–56) and his book, published in 1845, *Der Einzige und sein Eigentum*, was translated into English in 1907 as *The Ego and His Own*. I have made several efforts to read this book, but have continually found it incomprehensible. I used to excuse myself with the comment that the cult of the 'Ego' seemed to me as distasteful as Nietzsche's 'Superman', but anarchist admirers of Stirner assure me that his approach is quite different from Nietzsche's. They argue that Stirner's 'conscious egoism' does not in any way deny the human tendency towards altruistic behaviour, precisely because our own self-image is gratified by the way we perceive ourselves as social beings. They also draw my attention to Stirner's anticipation of the later perception by Robert Michels of an 'iron law of oligarchy', diagnosing an inbuilt tendency of all human institutions to ossify into oppressive bodies, which have to be opposed in the name of individual liberty.

Far more typical than Stirner of the anarchist individualist current was a long series of American activists and innovators, predating the vigorous history of anarchist propaganda among numerous immigrant groups of the late 19th and early 20th centuries: German, Russian, Jewish, Swedish, Dutch, Italian, and Spanish. Such guidebooks as James J. Martin's *Men Against the State* (which first appeared in 1953) and David DeLeon's *The American as Anarchist: Reflections on Indigenous Radicalism* (which first appeared in 1978) provide a rich and varied history in the United States of inventive individual and social anarchist argument and experiment.

The immigrant tradition was of social and collective ventures rapidly growing into deeply rooted organizations for welfare and conviviality. It included workers' unions, schools, and cooperatives. The indigenous tradition was far more individualistic but its protagonists have had a remarkable range of impacts on American life. Their chroniclers distinguish between the ideologies of these libertarians of the Left, and that of the libertarians of the Right. As David DeLeon separates them: 'While the libertarians of the Right despise the state because it hinders the freedom of property, Left libertarians condemn the state because it is a bastion of property.'

The first of these luminaries was Josiah Warren (1798–1874) who, disappointed by the failure of Robert Owen's cooperative colony of New Harmony, set up a Time Store in Cincinatti, whose customers bought goods in return for 'labour notes' promising the trader an equivalent product or service. This was followed by a cooperative Village of Equity in Ohio, the long-lived 'mutualist' village of Utopia, and the community of Modern Times on Long Island that similarly retained its cooperative character for at least 20 years. Warren's belief in the importance of the individual led him to advocate communal kitchens, to 'relieve the females of the family from the full, mill-horse drudgery to which they otherwise are irretrievably doomed'.

Lysander Spooner (1808–87) wanted an America of self-employed individuals sharing equal access to credit. He argued, too, that

> if a man has never consented or agreed to support a government, he breaks no faith in refusing to support it. And if he makes war on it, he does so as an open enemy, and not as a traitor.

Stephen Pearl Andrews (1812–86) similarly accepted that the sovereignty of the individual applied to *every* individual. Consequently, as Peter Marshall explains,

> He consistently opposed slavery and tried to free the state of Texas by raising money to buy off all of its slaves but the war with Mexico intervened. He also argued that sexual behaviour and family life should be matters of personal responsibility beyond the control of Church and State.

Like that of Warren, the individualism of S. P. Andrews led him to recommend communal nurseries, infant schools, and cooperative cafeterias, in order to liberate women.

Benjamin R. Tucker (1854–1939) was, in his day, the best-known of the American individualist anarchists, since his journal *Liberty* lasted a quarter of a century, until his Boston printing shop was burned down in 1907. He was also the pioneer translator of Proudhon and Bakunin.

But among the American libertarians of the 19th century, the most individual and the best remembered is Henry David Thoreau (1817–62). His famous book *Walden* is an account of the two years he spent seeking self-sufficiency in the hut he built for himself near Concord, Massachusetts. This did not imply a withdrawal from American life, for the man who declared that the soldier's natural enemy is the government that drills him was his country's most forthright subversive. One of his essays, usually called 'On the duty of civil disobedience', though originally published in 1849 as 'Resistance to civil government', attracted no attention at the time, but subsequently influenced both Tolstoy and Gandhi (who read it in prison in South Africa). Martin Luther King read it as a student in Atlanta, and recalled that,

> Fascinated by the idea of refusing to co-operate with an evil system, I was so deeply moved that I reread the work several times. This was my first intellectual contact with the theory of non-violent resistance.

Thoreau's essay on civil disobedience, originating in his sense of outrage at the United States' government's Mexican War and at the continuance of black slavery, began its history as a lecture to his fellow citizens at the Concord Lyceum in 1848. When the abolitionist John Brown took up arms against the United States in 1859 and was condemned to death, Thoreau, against some opposition, delivered an address in the Town Hall called 'A Plea for Captain John Brown'. Many decades later Havelock Ellis remarked that Thoreau was 'the *one man* in America to recognise the greatness of the occasion and to stand up publicly on his side'.

Another remarkable American individualist, Randolph Bourne (1886–1918), invented a famous phrase during the First World War, as he observed the process by which his country was manouevred into participating in that war. 'War is the *health* of the state', he claimed, and he explained that

> The State is the organisation of the herd to act offensively or defensively against another herd similarly organised. War sends the current of purpose and activity flowing down to the lowest level of the herd, and to its most remote branches. All the activities of society are linked together as fast as possible to this central purpose of making a military offensive or military defence, and the State

becomes what in peacetime it has vainly struggled to become . . .
The slack is taken up, the cross-currents fade out, and the nation
moves lumberingly and slowly, but with ever accelerated speed
and integration, towards the great end, towards that *peacefulness
of being at war* . . .

His perception of the way that 20th-century governments have
been able to manufacture and manipulate opinion is amply
demonstrated by events in the 90 years since he was writing.
American anarchist individualist protesters have lobbied in the
streets against the policies of the United States government ever
since. One was Ammon Hennacy, always described as 'the one-man
revolution', who maintained a continual individual protest against
United States imperialism, from the East Coast to the Southwest,
and another was Dorothy Day of the Catholic Worker Movement,
who testified for many decades of the 20th century to her faith in
self-organizing cooperative communities, which in political terms
has to be described as anarchism.

Some time later, in the 1970s, a series of books, from academics
rather than activists, proclaimed a different style of American
libertarianism. They were Robert Paul Wolff's *In Defense of
Anarchism*; Robert Nozick's *Anarchy, State and Utopia*;
David Friedman's *The Machinery of Freedom*; and Murray
Rothbard's *For a New Liberty: The Libertarian Manifesto*.
This phalanx of authors have provided the 'ideological
superstructure' of the swing to the Right in federal and local
politics in the United States, and in British politics for the aim
of 'rolling back the frontiers of the State', which was actually a
cloak for increased subservience to central decision-making.
Robert Paul Wolff claimed that 'philosophical anarchism would
seem to be the only reasonable belief for an enlightened man'.
Robert Nozick is said by the historian Peter Marshall to have
'helped to make libertarian and anarchist theory acceptable in
academic circles' – no small achievement; while David Friedman
has popularized for an American readership the argument of

Friedrich von Hayek that welfare legislation is the first step on *The Road to Serfdom*.

Peter Marshall sees the economist Murray Rothbard as the most aware of the actual anarchist tradition among the anarcho-capitalist apologists:

> He was originally regarded as an extreme right-wing Republican, but went on to edit La Boétie's libertarian classic *Of Voluntary Servitude* and now calls himself an anarchist. 'If you wish to know how the libertarians regard the State and any of its acts,' he wrote in *For a New Liberty*, 'simply think of the State as a criminal band, and all the libertarian attitudes will logically fall into place.' He reduces the libertarian creed to one central axiom, 'that no man or group of men may aggress against the person or property of anyone else.' Neither the State nor any private party therefore can initiate or threaten the use of force against any person for any purpose. Free individuals should regulate their affairs and dispose of their property only by voluntary agreement based on contractual obligation.

Rothbard is aware of a tradition, but he is singularly unaware of the old proverb that freedom for the pike means death for the minnow. For the bleak facts about the United States economy are that 10% of its citizens possess 85% of the nation's net wealth, and that this minority are also the people who benefit from every reduction in the nation's social welfare budget.

The libertarians of the Right have, nevertheless, a function in the spectrum of anarchist discussion. Every anarchist propagandist finds that the audience or readership is perplexed by the very idea that it might be possible to organize human life without government. That is why Kropotkin, as a libertarian of the Left, as we saw in Chapter 3, insisted that anarchist propagandists should identify new forms of organization for those functions that the state now fulfils through bureaucracy.

Murray Rothbard was one of the founders of a Libertarian Party in the United States, seeking, as Peter Marshall explains, to abolish 'the entire Federal regulatory apparatus as well as social security, welfare, public education and taxation', and urging the United States 'to withdraw from the United Nations and its foreign commitments, and to reduce its military forces to those required for minimal defence.'

Beyond an aspiration to repeal all 'victimless crime' laws, we did not learn about any commitment to a change in the United States penal system, which now imprisons a larger proportion of the population than any other nation that keeps reliable records. But in any case, the other philosophers of the new libertarian Right seem to have a less sweeping agenda. Robert Paul Wolff, for example, in the 1998 reprint of his book *In Defense of Anarchism*, suggests that 'a system of in-the-home voting machines be set up', each of them 'attached to the television set', to decide social and political issues. He asserts that 'social justice would flourish as it has never flourished before'.

Most anarchists would see this as a rather pathetic evasion of the issues raised by the anarchist criticism of American society, and would prefer to commemorate a far richer heritage of dissent in the United States, exemplified by a long series of well-remembered propagandists, from Thoreau in one generation and Emma Goldman in another, down to Paul Goodman, who bequeathed an intriguing legacy to his anarchist successors. In his last article in the American press, he suggested that

> For me, the chief principle of anarchism is not freedom but autonomy, the ability to initiate a task and do it one's own way. The weakness of 'my' anarchism is that the lust for freedom is a powerful motive for political change, whereas autonomy is not. Autonomous people protect themselves stubbornly but by less strenuous means, including plenty of passive resistance. They do it their own way anyway. The pathos of oppressed people, however, is that, if they break free, they don't know what to do. Not having been

> autonomous, they don't know what it's like, and before they learn,
> they have new managers who are not in a hurry to abdicate . . .

The 19th-century American individualists were busy creating
communes, cooperatives, alternative schools, local currencies,
and schemes for mutual banking. They were busy social inventors
exploring the potential of autonomy, including women's liberation
and black equality. Their experience, in the social climate of
America, illustrates Martin Buber's insistence, cited in Chapter 3,
on the inverse relationship between the social principle and the
political principle. The practice of autonomy generates the
experience that enlarges the possibility of success. Or as the
American anarchist David Wieck expresssed it: 'The habit of direct
action is, perhaps, identical with the habit of being free, prepared to
live responsibly in a free society.'

The American 'libertarians' of the 20th century are academics
rather than social activists, and their inventiveness seems to be
limited to providing an ideology for untrammelled market
capitalism.

Chapter 8
Quiet revolutions

The gulf between anarchist aspirations and the actual history of the 20th century could be seen as an indication of the folly of impossible hopes, but for the concurrent failure of other political ideologies of the Left. Which of us was not profoundly relieved by the collapse of Soviet communism, even though we have had little reason to rejoice in subsequent regimes? As the penal settlements slowly emptied of their survivors, the true believers were obliged to question their assumptions.

Many years ago, the American journalist Dwight Macdonald wrote an article on 'Politics Past' which included a long footnote that he later told me was the most-quoted paragraph he had ever written. His footnote said:

> The revolutionary alternative to the *status quo* today is not collectivised property administered by a 'workers' state' whatever *that* means, but some kind of anarchist decentralisation that will break up mass society into small communities where individuals can live together as variegated human beings instead of as impersonal units in the mass sum. The shallowness of the New Deal and the British Labour Party's post-war regime is shown by their failure to improve any of the important things in people's lives – the actual relationships on the job, the way they spend their leisure, and child-rearing and sex and art. It is mass living that vitiates all these today,

and the State that holds together the *status quo*. Marxism glorifies 'the masses' and endorses the State. Anarchism leads back to the individual and the community, which is 'impractical' but necessary – that is to say, it is revolutionary.

In a partial, incomplete, but visible way, several of the revolutions he sought have already transformed the surface of life. To take an example that is by definition superficial, one that is obvious and visible but seldom discussed, consider the revolution in dress in the second half of the 20th century. Fifty years ago in Britain, the social class of men, women, and children could be recognized from their clothing. Today this is no longer true, except for the tiny minority who can read the signs of expensive and exclusive dress. This is usually attributed to the growth of mass production and the fact that the garment trade is the first route to the global economy for a low-paid workforce in the 'developing' world. But it has more to do with the relaxation of dress codes, pioneered all through the 20th century by the radical nonconformists' rejection of fashion.

The ignoring of dress codes based on occupation or social class was a small and personal rebuff to convention. But of course a far more significant revolution, gaining ground all through the century, has been the women's movement, rejecting the universal convention of male dominance. Among its anarchist pioneers was Emma Goldman, with her trenchant pamphlet on *The Tragedy of Women's Emancipation*, arguing that the vote, which had failed to liberate men, was not likely to free women. Emancipation, she argued, must come from the woman herself,

> First, by asserting herself as a personality, and not a sex commodity. Second, by refusing the right to anyone over her body; by refusing to bear children, unless she wants them; by refusing to be a servant to God, the State, society, the husband, the family etc., by making her life simpler, but deeper and richer. That is, by trying to learn the meaning and substance of life in all its complexities, by freeing

herself from the fear of public opinion and public condemnation. Only that, and not the ballot, will set women free . . .

It was among the anarchists that the habit began of what were called 'free unions' as opposed to marriages licensed by church or state. Today these are almost as common as regular marriages, with the result that the stigma once associated with illegitimacy has, during the century, disappeared. This change was, of course, accelerated by the pharmacological revolution of the contraceptive pill.

Alex Comfort (1920–2000) was a physician, novelist, poet, and anarchist. His lectures to meetings of the London Anarchist Group in the late 1940s gave rise to his book *Barbarism and Sexual Freedom*, published by Freedom Press in 1948 at a time when no 'respectable' publisher would issue such a book. This in turn led to his *Sexual Behaviour in Society* and to his phenomenally successful manuals on sex. In his book *More Joy: A Lovemaking Companion to The Joy of Sex* (1973), he included an anarchist account of the connection between sexuality and politics. He asserted that

> acquiring the awareness and the attitudes which can come from good sexual experience does not make for selfish withdrawal: it is more inclined to radicalise people. The anti-sexualism of authoritarian societies and the people who run them does not spring from conviction (they themselves have sex), but from the vague perception that freedom here might lead to a liking for freedom elsewhere. People who have eroticised their experience of themselves and the world are, on the one hand, inconveniently unwarlike, and on the other, violently combative in resisting political salesmen and racists who threaten the personal freedom they have attained and want to see others share.

Comfort hoped that his books would provide both reassurance and liberation, and that they would be a contribution to another 20th-century revolution: that of the relationships between parents and children. It is hard to imagine in today's Western Europe the punitive behaviour of parents towards children that was taken for granted a century ago.

The same is true of the relationships between teachers and children. The recollections of people who were schoolchildren in the first decade of the 20th century are full of accounts of the physical punishment they received or that they continually feared. In the century's last decade a law in Britain banned corporal punishment in schools. This was not a sudden legal decision. It reflected the influence of a handful of 'progressive' schools on general educational thinking.

Many observers claim that the school system has failed to prepare for the dilemmas that came in the wake of the abandonment of physical punishment. The teacher is deprived of the weapon that was seen as the ultimate sanction of the school. This has resulted in increased numbers of children being excluded from school because teachers have declined to have them in the class. Anyone who has observed how one disruptive member of the class can make learning impossible for the whole group has no criticism to make of those teachers (especially since their employers put pressure on them not to upset statistics).

In the 1960s and 1970s an intriguing situation arose in several British cities: London, Liverpool, Leeds, and Glasgow. Groups of enthusiasts found empty buildings and set up 'free schools' to provide an informal education for children who were either excluded from school or had excluded themselves through truancy. (One of them, White Lion Free School in London, lasted from 1972 to 1990.) The regime of these schools was consciously modelled on the experience of the progressive school movement. I asked a veteran of those experiments why the idea had not been revived among the new generation of excluded children at the start of the new century. She gave me two reasons: first, the legal requirement in Britain for all schools to teach the National Curriculum introduced during the Thatcher regime and retained by its successors; and second, the difficulty of finding premises that would meet the safety and sanitary regulations prescribed for schools. However, it is hard to imagine returning to the regime of fear that governed schools a century ago. The quiet revolution in education can only move forward.

Two other changes in Britain from the 1960s also seem irreversible. One is the removal of the fear of criminal prosecution for homosexuality. This had been recommended in a government report commissioned from John Wolfenden and published in 1957, but years of argument and agitation were needed to engineer a change in the law. The other was the ending of capital punishment in 1965. On the eve of the debate that brought this change, the anarchist publishers Freedom Press presented every Member of Parliament with a copy of their edition of Charles Duff's devastating book, *A Handbook on Hanging*, which took the form of an enthusiastic manual for executioners. Only very humourless observers would complain that support for campaigns to end barbaric laws was a contradiction of the anarchist anti-parliamentary stance.

Taken together, the social changes in Britain that I have listed are an indication that while the anarchists have made little progress towards the large-scale changes in society that they hoped to bring about, they have contributed to a long series of small liberations that have lifted a huge load of human misery.

Several anarchist groups sought to link together these struggles for human liberation into a conscious campaign with a wider relevance. In the Netherlands, the Provos introduced games and playful alternatives to ridicule the official city management. Their most famous ploy was to litter Amsterdam with white bicycles for public use, to demonstrate that cars were unnecessary. They were followed by the Kabouters, or gnomes, forerunners of the Green movement. One of them, Roel van Duyn, made the same links between anarchism and cybernetics, the science of control and communication systems, that had been suggested by the founder of cybernetics, the neurologist Grey Walter. He had pointed out that

> We find no boss in the brain, no oligarchic ganglion or glandular Big Brother. Within our heads our very lives depend on equality of opportunity, on specialisation with versatility, on free communication and just restraint, a freedom without interference. Here too, local minorities can and do control their own means of production and expression in free and equal intercourse with their neighbours.

Among French attempts to sharpen the widespread vaguely libertarian trends were the Situationists, notably Raoul Vaneigem with his manifesto on *The Revolution of Everyday Life* (1967). As Peter Marshall puts it:

> The way out for the Situationists was not to wait for a distant revolution but to reinvent daily life here and now. To transform the perception of the world and to change the structure of society is the same thing. By liberating oneself, one changed power relations and therefore transformed society . . .

The Situationists, like the Kabouters, have passed into history without managing to transform society, but France and the Netherlands, like Britain, have seen a series of modest gains in civilization.

Then the quiet revolution became noisier as, thanks to the Internet, the anarchists were linked to a variety of anti-capitalist protesters in a series of large-scale demonstrations whenever global bodies met to advance their interests. George Monbiot, in his book *Captive State*, describes how

> In April 1998, a ragged band of protesters inflicted the first of a series of defeats on a coalition of the most powerful interests on earth. The 29 richest nations had joined forces with the world's

biggest multinational companies to write 'the constitution of a single global economy'. Proposed and drafted by businessmen, secretly discussed by governments, the Multilateral Agreement on Investment would, had it succeeded, have granted corporations the right to sue any country whose laws restricted their ability to make money. The treaty was, its opponents claimed, a charter for the corporate takeover of the world.

Monbiot explains how the leaking of this secret treaty in 1997 led to objectors posting the details on the Web, guaranteeing demonstrations wherever the governmental negotiators might meet. Public pressure and internal disputes obliged the global leaders to abandon their negotiations, only to revive them under the auspices of the World Trade Organization. Its negotiators met in Seattle in November 1999, but the talks there collapsed as tens of thousands of people from around the world protested outside, in the name of the poor countries and the planet's environment.

In the string of demonstrations that began at Seattle, the techniques adopted by the Provos and Kabouters were used to ridicule the forces of law and order. Sean Sheehan, in his account of contemporary anarchism, describes the scene in Prague, a year after Seattle, where in demonstrations against the International Monetary Fund,

> mini armies of protesters came dressed as fairies and armed with feather dusters to tickle the ranks of heavily clothed, armed police. At such protests, lines of transport tend to be blocked not so much by burning barricades and street battles but by giant contraptions like the Liberation Puppet, capable of snarling up a major highway.

But after five days of protest had brought a World Trade Organization conference close to collapse, the heavily armed police responded. As Sheehan reports,

That the size and organisation of the protests spooked the police into frenzied and blatantly illegal behaviour was confirmed by the fact that of the 631 arrests, only 14 ever went to trial.

Having started gently and humorously, the big international demonstrations of opposition to global capitalism are no longer quiet revolutions. There seems to have been a pact between the world's police forces to escalate the violence of their response to demonstrators. Sean Sheehan goes on to record that

'Normal' police violence at Seattle escalated at the anti-capitalism protest in Gothenburg in June 2001 to the issuing of live ammunition to the police with three people shot. When another anti-capitalist protest was mounted in Genoa in July, the event turned into a violent riot, with armoured vans driving at speed into crowds of protesters and a late-night, cold-blooded and very violent assault by the police on a building where media activists and their material were lodged.

One young anarchist was killed at Genoa, and his death prompted a renewed discussion of strategies of protest. Maybe there are subtler ways of undermining global capitalism? The quiet revolutionaries who transformed the culture of Western countries in the 20th century have not yet discovered them.

Chapter 9
The federalist agenda

A frequent criticism of anarchism is that it is an ideology that fits a
world of isolated villages, small enough to be self-governing entities,
but not the global, multi-national society that we all inhabit in real
life. But in fact the major anarchist thinkers of the past: Proudhon,
Bakunin, and Kropotkin, had a federalist agenda that was a
foretaste of modern debates on European unity.

That minority of children in any European country who were given
the opportunity of studying the history of Europe as well as that of
their own nations learned that there were two great events in the
19th century: the unification of Germany, achieved by Bismarck and
the Emperor Wilhelm I; and the unification of Italy, won by Cavour,
Mazzini, Garibaldi, and Vittorio Emanuale II. These triumphs had
been welcomed by the whole world (which in those days meant the
European world) because Germany and Italy had left behind all
those silly little principalities, republics, papal provinces, and city
states, to become nation states, empires, and, of course, conquerors.

They had become like France, whose little local despots were finally
unified by force, first by Louis XIV with his majestic slogan '*L'État
c'est moi*', and then by Napoleon, heir to the *Grande Revolution*, just
like Stalin in the 20th century, who built up the administrative
machinery of terror to ensure that the slogan was true. Or they had
become like England, whose kings (and its one republican ruler,

Oliver Cromwell) had conquered the Welsh, Scots, and Irish, and sought to dominate the rest of the world outside Europe. The same thing was happening at the other end of Europe. Ivan IV, appropriately named 'The Terrible', conquered central Asia as far as the Pacific, and Peter I, known as 'The Great', using the techniques he had learned in France and Britain, took over the Baltic, most of Poland, and the west of Ukraine.

Advanced opinion throughout Europe welcomed Germany and Italy to the gentleman's club of national and imperial powers. The eventual results in the 20th century were appalling adventures in conquest, with the devastating loss of life among young men from the villages of Europe in the two world wars, and the rise of populist demagogues like Hitler and Mussolini, as well as their endless imitators to this day, who claim *L'État c'est moi*. Consequently, although we have had all too few politicians arguing for the breakdown of nations, we have a host of them of every persuasion who have sought European unity: economic, social, administrative, or, of course, political.

Needless to say, in efforts for unification promoted by politicians we have a multitude of administrators in Brussels issuing edicts about which varieties of vegetable seeds, or what constituents of beefburgers or ice cream, may be sold in the shops of member nations. The newspapers joyfully report all this trivia. The press gives far less attention to another undercurrent of pan-European opinion, evolving from the views expressed in Strasbourg from people of every political hue, claiming the existence of a 'Europe of the Regions', and daring to argue that the nation state was a phenomenon of the 16th to 19th centuries, which will not have any useful future in the 21st century. The forthcoming pattern of administration in the federated Europe that they are struggling to discover is a link between, let us say, Calabria, Wales, Andalusia, Aquitaine, Galicia, or Saxony, as *regions*, rather than as *nations*, seeking their regional identity, economically and culturally, which has been lost in their incorporation in nation states, where the centre of gravity is elsewhere.

In the great tide of nationalism in the 19th century there was a handful of prophetic and dissenting voices, urging the alternative of federalism. It is interesting, at least, that those whose names survive were the three best-known anarchist thinkers of that century. The political Left as it evolved in the 20th century has dismissed their legacy as irrelevant. So much the worse for the Left, since the debate is now monopolized by the political Right, which has its own agenda in opposing both federalism and regionalism.

First among these anarchist precursors was Proudhon, who devoted two of his books to the idea of federation in opposition to that of the nation state. They were *La Fédération et l'Unité en Italie* of 1862, and in the following year his *Du Principe Fédératif*. Proudhon was French, a citizen of a unified, centralized nation state, with the result that he was obliged to become a refugee in Belgium. And he feared the unification of Italy on several different levels. In his book *De la Justice* of 1858, he had forecast that the creation of the German Empire would bring only trouble both to the Germans and to the rest of Europe, and he pursued this argument into the political history of Italy.

On the bottom level was history, where natural factors like geology and climate had shaped local customs and attitudes. 'Italy', he claimed,

> is federal by the constitution of her territory; by the diversity of her inhabitants; in the nature of her genius; in her mores; in her history. She is federal in all her being and has been since all eternity . . . And by federation you will make her as many times free as you give her independent states.

It was therefore unnatural for Italy to become a nation state.

He understood that Cavour and Napoleon III had agreed to make a federal Italy, but he knew they would rely on a vainglorious princeling from the House of Savoy who would settle for nothing less than a centralized constitutional monarchy. And beyond this, he profoundly mistrusted the liberal anti-clericalism of Mazzini, not through any love of the Papacy but because he recognized that Mazzini's slogan '*Dio e popolo*' could be exploited by any demagogue who could seize the machinery of a centralized state. He saw that the existence of this administrative machinery was an absolute threat to personal and local liberty. Proudhon was almost alone among 19th-century political theorists to perceive this:

> Liberal today under a liberal government, it will tomorrow become the formidable engine of a usurping despot. It is a perpetual temptation to the executive power, a perpetual threat to the people's liberties. No rights, individual or collective, can be sure of a future. Centralisation might, then, be called the disarming of a nation for the profit of its government . . .

Everything we now know about the 20th-century history of Europe, Asia, Latin America, or Africa supports this perception. Nor does the North American style of federalism, so lovingly conceived by Thomas Jefferson and his friends, guarantee the removal of this threat. One of Proudhon's English biographers, Edward Hyams, comments that

> it has become apparent since the Second World War that United States Presidents can and do make use of the Federal administrative machine in a way which makes a mockery of democracy.

And his Canadian translator Richard Vernon paraphrases Proudhon's conclusion thus:

> Solicit men's views in the mass, and they will return stupid, fickle and violent answers; solicit their views as members of definite groups with real solidarity and a distinctive character, and their answers will be responsible and wise. Expose them to the political

'language' of mass democracy, which represents 'the people' as unitary and undivided, and minorities as traitors, and they will give birth to tyranny; expose them to the political language of federalism, in which the people figures as a diversified aggregate of real associations, and they will resist tyranny to the end.

This observation reveals a profound understanding of the psychology of politics. Proudhon was extrapolating from the evolution of the Swiss Confederation, but Europe has other examples in a whole series of specialist fields. The Netherlands has a reputation for its mild or lenient penal policy. The official explanation of this is the replacement in 1886 of the Code Napoleon by 'a genuine Dutch criminal code' based upon cultural traditions like 'the well-known Dutch "tolerance" and tendency to accept deviant minorities'. I am quoting the Netherlands criminologist Dr Willem de Haan, who cites the explanation that Dutch society

has traditionally been based upon religious, political and ideological rather than class lines. The important denominational groupings created their own social institutions in all major public spheres. This process . . . is responsible for transforming a pragmatic, tolerant general attitude into an absolute social *must*.

In other words it is *diversity* and not unity that creates the kind of society in which you and I can most comfortably live. And modern Dutch attitudes are rooted in the diversity of the medieval city states of Holland and Zeeland, which demonstrates, as much as Proudhon's regionalism, that a desirable future for all Europe lies in an accommodation of local differences.

Discussions about European integration in the 1860s prompted a sceptical reaction from Proudhon:

Among French democrats there has been much talk of a European confederation, or a United States of Europe. By this they seem to understand nothing but an alliance of all the states which presently exist in Europe, great and small, presided over by a permanent congress. It is taken for granted that each state will retain the form of government that suits it best. Now since each state will have votes in the congress in proportion to its population and territory, the small states in this so-called confederation will soon be incorporated into the large ones . . .

Swallowing up neighbouring countries may be unfashionable nowadays, but we can see Proudhon's misgivings being realized in the way debates and decisions of the European Community are dominated by the large states at the expense of the smaller member nations.

The second of my 19th-century mentors, Michael Bakunin, demands our attention for a variety of reasons. He was almost alone among that century's political thinkers in foreseeing the horrors of the clash of modern nation states in the First and Second World Wars, as well as predicting the results of centralizing Marxism in the Russian Empire. In 1867 Prussia and France seemed to be poised for a war about who should control Luxembourg and this, through the network of interests and alliances, 'threatened to engulf all Europe'. A League for Peace and Freedom held its congress in Geneva, sponsored by prominent people from various countries, such as Giuseppe Garibaldi, Victor Hugo, and John Stuart Mill. Bakunin seized the opportunity to address this audience, and published his opinions under the title *Fédéralisme, Socialisme, et Anti-Théologisme*. This document set out 13 points on which, according to Bakunin, the Geneva Congress was unanimous.

The first of these points proclaimed

> That in order to achieve the triumph of liberty, justice and peace in the international relations of Europe, and to render civil war impossible among the various peoples which make up the European family, only a single course lies open: to constitute the *United States of Europe*.

His second point argued that this aim implied that states must be replaced by regions, for it observed

> That the formation of these States of Europe can never come about between the States as constituted at present, in view of the monstrous disparity which exists between their various powers.

His fourth point claimed

> That not even if it called itself a republic could any centralised, bureaucratic and by the same token militarist State enter seriously and genuinely into an international federation. By virtue of its constitution, which will always be an explicit or implicit denial of domestic liberty, it would necessarily imply a declaration of permanent war and a threat to the existence of neighbouring countries.

Consequently his fifth point demanded

> That all the supporters of the League should therefore bend all their energies towards the reconstruction of their various countries, in order to replace the old organisation founded throughout upon violence and the principle of authority by a new organisation based solely upon the interests, needs and inclinations of the populace, and owning no principle other than that of the free federation of individuals into communes, communes into provinces, provinces into nations, and the latter into the United States, first of Europe, then of the whole world.

The vision thus became bigger and bigger, but Bakunin was careful to include the acceptance of secession. His eighth point declared that

> Just because a region has formed part of a State, even by voluntary accession, it by no means follows that it incurs any obligation to remain tied to it for ever. No obligation in perpetuity is acceptable

to human justice . . . The right of free union and equally free secession comes first and foremost among all political rights; without it, confederation would be nothing but centralisation in disguise.

Bakunin refers admiringly to the Swiss Confederation, 'practising federation so successfully today', as he put it, and Proudhon too explicitly took as a model the Swiss supremacy of the *commune* as the unit of social organization, linked by the *canton*, with a purely administrative *federal council*. But both remembered the events of 1848, when the *Sonderbund* of secessionist cantons were compelled by war to accept the new constitution of the majority. Proudhon and Bakunin agreed in condemning this subversion of federalism by the unitary principle. There must be a right of secession.

Switzerland, precisely because of its decentralized structure, was a refuge for numerous political refugees from the Austro-Hungarian, German, and Russian empires. One Russian anarchist was even expelled from Switzerland: he was too much even for the Swiss Federal Council. This was Peter Kropotkin, whose ideas connect 19th-century federalism with 20th-century regional geography.

Kropotkin's youth was spent as an army officer in geological expeditions in the Far Eastern provinces of the Russian Empire. His autobiography tells of the outrage he felt to see how central administration and funding destroyed any improvement of local conditions, through ignorance, incompetence, and universal corruption, and through the destruction of ancient communal institutions which might have enabled people to change their own lives. The rich got richer, the poor got poorer, and the administrative machinery was suffocated by boredom and embezzlement. There is a similar literature from any other empire or nation state.

In 1872 Kropotkin made his first visit to Western Europe, and in Switzerland was intoxicated by the air of democracy, even a bourgeois one. In the Jura hills he stayed with the watch-makers, a community of self-employed craftsmen. His biographer Martin Miller describes his reactions:

> Kropotkin's meetings and talks with the workers on their jobs revealed the kind of spontaneous freedom without authority or direction from above that he had dreamed about. Isolated and self-sufficient, the Jura watchmakers impressed Kropotkin as an example that could transform society if such a community were allowed to develop on a large scale. There was no doubt in his mind that this community would work because it was not a matter of imposing an artificial 'system' such as had been attempted by Muraviev in Siberia but of permitting the natural activity of the workers to function according to their own interests.

His stay in the Jura hills was a turning point for Kropotkin. The rest of his life was, in a sense, devoted to gathering the evidence for anarchism, federalism, and regionalism.

Kropotkin's approach is not simply a matter of academic history. In a study of *Un federalista Russo, Pietro Kropotkine* (1922), the Italian anarchist Camillo Berneri quotes the 'Letter to the Workers of Western Europe' that Kropotkin handed to the British Labour Party politician Margaret Bondfield in June 1920. In the course of it he declared that:

> Imperial Russia is dead and will never be revived. The future of the various provinces which composed the Empire will be directed towards a large federation. The natural territories of the different sections of this federation are in no way distinct from those with which we are familiar in the history of Russia, of its ethnography and economic life. All the attempts to bring together the consituent parts of the Russian Empire, such as Finland, the Baltic provinces, Lithuania, Ukraine, Georgia, Armenia, Siberia and others, under a central authority are doomed to failure. The future of what was the Russian Empire is directed towards a federation of independent units.

Today we can see the relevance of this opinion, ignored for 70 years. As an exile in Western Europe, Kropotkin had close contact with a range of pioneers of regional thinking. The relationship between regionalism and anarchism has been handsomely delineated by the geographer Peter Hall, when director of the Institute of Urban and Regional Development at Berkeley, California, in his book *Cities of Tomorrow* (1988). There was Kropotkin's fellow anarchist geographer Elisée Reclus, arguing for small-scale human societies based on the ecology of their regions. There was Paul Vidal de la Blache, another founder of French geography, who argued that 'the region was more than an object of survey; it was to provide the basis for the total reconstruction of social and political life'. For Vidal, as Professor Hall explains, it was the region, not the nation, which

> as the motor force of human development; the almost sensual reciprocity between men and women and their surroundings, was the seat of comprehensible liberty and the mainspring of cultural evolution, which were being attacked and eroded by the centralised nation-state and by large-scale machine industry.

Finally there was the extraordinary Scottish biologist Patrick Geddes, who tried to encapsulate all these regionalist ideas, whether geographical, social, historical, political, or economic, into an ideology of reasons for regions, known to most of us through the work of his disciple Lewis Mumford.

Professor Hall pointed out that

> many, though by no means all, of the early visions of the planning movement stemmed from the anarchist movement, which flourished in the last decades of the nineteenth century and the first years of the twentieth . . . The vision of these anarchist pioneers was not merely of an alternative built form, but of an alternative society, nether capitalist nor bureaucratic-socialist: a society based on voluntary co-operation among men and women, working and living in small self-governing communities.

Those 19th-century anarchist thinkers were a century in advance of their contemporaries in warning the peoples of Europe of the consequences of not adopting a regionalist and federalist approach. After every kind of disastrous experience in the 20th century, the rulers of the nation states of Europe have directed policy towards several kinds of supranational entities. The crucial issue that faces them is whether to conceive of a Europe of States or a Europe of Regions.

To do them justice, the advocates of a united Europe have developed a doctrine of 'subsidiarity', by which governmental decisions outside the remit of the supranational institutions of the European Community should be taken by regional or local levels of administration, rather than by national governments. A resolution has been adopted by the Council of Europe, calling for national governments to adopt its *Charter for Local Self-Government*, 'to formalise commitment to the principle that government functions should be carried out at the lowest level possible and only transferred to higher government by consent.'

This precept is an extraordinary tribute to Proudhon, Bakunin, and Kropotkin and the ideas that they were alone in voicing (apart from some interesting Spanish thinkers like Pi y Margall or Joaquin Costa). Of course it is one of the first aspects of pan-European ideology that national governments will choose to ignore, though there are obvious differences between various nation states in this respect. In many of them, for example Germany, Italy, Spain, and even France, the machinery of government is considerably more devolved than it was 50 years ago. The same is true of the former Soviet Union.

One anarchist thinker from the Netherlands, Thom Holterman, has set out the criteria which anarchists would see as the prerequisites for a free united Europe. His warning is precisely that the obstacle to a Europe of the Regions is the existence of nation states. Another is that because the thinking and planning of the future of Europe is in the hands of governmental bureaucracies, they are all preparing for a Europe of the bureaucrats.

Kropotkin used to cite the lifeboat institution as an example of the kind of voluntary and non-coercive organization envisaged by anarchists that could provide a worldwide service without the principle of authority intervening. Two other examples of the way in which local groups and associations could combine to provide a complex network of functions without any central authority are the post office and the railways. You can post a letter to Chile or China, confident that it will get there, as a result of freely-arrived-at agreements between different national post offices, without there being any central world postal authority at all. Or you can travel across Europe and Asia over the lines of a dozen different railway systems, public and private, without any kind of central railway authority. Coordination requires neither uniformity nor bureaucracy.

Chapter 10

Green aspirations and anarchist futures

When Kropotkin's *Fields, Factories and Workshops* first appeared in 1899, the precursors of the Green movement found it an inspiration, since its author stressed the productivity of small-scale decentralized industry, and of a 'horticultural' approach to food production, for its immense output. When his book was re-issued at the end of the First World War, an added preliminary note observed that: 'It pleads for a new economy in the energies used in supplying the needs of human life, since these needs are increasing and the energies are not inexhaustible.'

In those days this was a rare recognition of the limits to growth. Today we have a vast literature on the problems of resource depletion and environmental destruction. The difficulty for environmental activists, trying to enlist the support of fellow citizens, is one of priorities: which campaign most urgently needs a helping hand? Capitalism roams the globe, seeking the least protected labour market and the least protected physical environment, in order to stimulate, and to win, an ever-growing market for its goods. It describes this process as 'consumer sovereignty' and thus evades any responsibility for its ruthless exploitation of poor people and weak economies. The richer we are, the more we are inclined to shrug off our share of this responsibility.

For many years now, we in the rich economies have had a series of movements and campaigns described in general terms as 'environmental', 'conservationist', or 'green', or even 'ecological', drawing our attention to the crises of the environment, global warming, and the depletion of finite resources. Critics of these campaigns in the rich world point out that they do not always include an awareness of the plight of the rich world's poor. Amartya Sen remarked on the paradox that 'In the poor world the poor are thin and the rich are fat. In the rich world the rich are thin and the poor are fat.' He is the author of a famous study of who eats and who starves, and of *what* they eat, with a theory of 'entitlements', defining these as the set of 'alternative commodity bundles which a person can command'. His observation is a reminder that in every society there are several simultaneous food cultures, ultimately determined by levels of poverty and affluence. In the poor world the powerful and wealthy and their military elites live grandly, while the poor are ill-nourished and sometimes starving. In the rich world a significant poor minority lives on the 'junk food' that the affluent can afford to despise. In Britain the number of children growing up in poverty trebled between 1968 and 1998.

Any discussion of environmental issues has to start with the fact of malnutrition in a world of plenty, and then proceed to examine the high cost of the rich world's 'cheap' food. Kropotkin's arguments included the claim that a densely populated small country like Britain could feed itself from its own land, an idea regarded as absurd even though it was based on European experience. A century later I had the pleasure of meeting Jac Smit, president of the Urban Agriculture Network and co-author of the United Nations report on *Urban Agriculture: Food, Jobs and Sustainable Cities*, who explained how in Chinese cities 90% of vegetables are locally grown, and that

> Hong Kong, the densest large city in the world, produces within its boundaries two-thirds of the poultry, one-sixth of the pigs, and close to half the vegetables eaten by its citizens and visitors.

The best-known examples of urban intensive food production are provided by the vast cities of South-East Asia. Singapore's 1,500 hectares of 'agro-technology parks' are famous. As their admirer Geoff Wilson points out,

> The inescapable logic is that while rural agriculture can need up to eight fossil fuel energy units to produce one food energy unit sold in supermarkets, urban agriculture can provide up to eight food energy units for every one fossil fuel energy unit.

Tim Lang, a professor of food policy who has been concerned for years with the implications of findings like these, reminds us that

> Supermarket distribution systems are totally dependent upon cheap energy. Far from being more convenient, hypermarkets are actually making us make more, not less, shopping trips. The average number increased by 28 per cent between 1978 and 1991. Shoppers also have to go further: the distance rose by 60 per cent between 1978 and 1991 ... The common factor to all this is the food retailers' use of centralised distribution systems. Each firm has its own regional distribution centres (RDCs). All food goes to the RDC and thence to the shops. As a result the food travels much further ...

This is known as the food-miles issue. It has been extended to even more bizarre lengths by the policies of the giant food retailers, searching the globe for suppliers who are cheapest, regardless of the diversion of local water supplies from meeting traditional local needs. In my nearest town in East Anglia I can buy Mexican carrots, Australian onions, African mange-tout peas, and Peruvian asparagus. This fact contributes far more to global warming than my careless use of electricity. Professor John Houghton, Chairman of the Royal Commission on Environmental Pollution and of the United Nations Advisory Panel on Climate Change, thought there was something absurd in the fact that he had eaten delicious new potatoes for his lunch. They had been delivered by a 40-tonne lorry to his local hypermarket after being flown by superjet to England.

And, as he commented, 'I could have grown them in my own back garden.'

His remark was important because it illustrates the gulf between our green aspirations and our actual behaviour. In exploring this gap, the work of the American anarchist Murray Bookchin has been significant and influential. He, like Rachel Carson, had been a propagandist on environmental issues in the 1950s and 1960s, and this gave him the same kind of forerunner status in the emerging American Green movement. He linked this with the home-grown American anarchist tradition. 'What we are trying to do', he explained,

> is to redeem certain aspects of the American Dream. There are, of course, several American dreams: one is the John Wayne tradition of the cowboy going out to the West, and the whole notion of pioneering individualism; another is the immigrant American dream, this being the land of opportunity where the streets are made of gold. But there is a *third* American dream, which is the oldest of the lot, dating back to Puritan times, which stresses community, decentralisation, self-sufficiency, mutual aid and face-to-face democracy.

This is where Bookchin came into conflict with yet another American dream. As ecological awareness spread among the children of the affluent, the national guilt over the genocide of indigenous peoples led to an exaltation of the Noble Savage, and a distaste for ordinary mortals who hadn't got the Message. What was seen as 'Deep Ecology' became fashionable among those affluent enough to 'get away from it all' and pursue every kind of mystical belief, so long as the cheques kept flowing into their bank accounts. Many of Bookchin's fellow citizens shifted from an involvement in social issues to a sentimental and privileged idealization of 'wilderness' and the natural environment, with a consequent misanthropy towards their fellow humans.

Bookchin's vigorous repudiation of these approaches has sought to confront the abandonment of social concerns in an increasingly divided America, re-asserting the claims of 'Social Ecology' and aiming, as he said, to advance 'a serious challenge to society with its vast, hierarchical, sexist, class-ruled, state apparatus and militaristic history'.

Most anarchists would take it for granted that an ecologically viable society is incompatible with capitalism and its demand for continually expanding markets, achieved through the invention of wants and the built-in obsolescence of consumer goods. At the same time, most of us feel that in seeking more ecologically viable ways of living, we cannot wait until the downfall of the capitalist system. The Green movement has been in existence long enough for its adherents to learn which approaches are most relevant *for them*.

In the 1970s I was lucky enough to be employed to start a journal for teachers and students called the *Bulletin of Environmental Education* (BEE). One of its most stimulating mentors was an inventive young man called Peter Harper, who in 1975 went to Wales to join a group of enthusiasts who were starting the Centre for Alternative Technology (CAT) at Machynlleth, in an old quarry in a landscape of industrial dereliction. By the end of the century that enterprise (operating as a workers' cooperative of 28 members) was being visited by about 80,000 people every year, including 20,000 children, and is world-famous as a demonstration site for environmentally friendly power generation, building construction, and sewage disposal. I am told that it generates 90% of its own energy requirements in renewable form from sun, wind, and water.

Since he has long practical experience in this field, I take Peter Harper's conclusions seriously. He told interviewers in 1998 that

The craze for self-sufficiency and small-is-beautiful has passed. Don't try to do it all yourself. Start where you are strong, not where you are weak ... Don't try to *make* your energy: try to *save* your energy. Most of the action is going to be in cities, where the majority of humans will soon be living and where, contrary to our old Arcadian assumptions, sustainable modern lifestyles are more easily achieved.

His continual probing of the environmental consciousness of our fellow citizens has led him to make a different distinction from that between Deep Ecologists and Social Ecologists. Peter Harper divides us into Light Greens (with more money than time) and Deep Greens (with, perhaps, more time than money). The Light Greens, he suggests, are involved with the new technology of solar heating, fuel-efficient lightweight motor cars, and sustainable consumption, while the Deep Greens believe in small, insulated houses, bicycles and public transport, home-grown food, repair and recycling, local currency schemes, and barter.

Meanwhile, the rest of society will continue to belong to the culture of *MORE!* For, as he observes,

People aspire to greater convenience and comfort, more personal space, easy mobility, a sense of expanding possibilities. This is the modern consumerist project: what modern societies are all about. It is a central feature of mainstream politics and economics that consumerist aspirations are not seriously challenged. On the contrary, the implied official message is 'Hang on in there: we will deliver.' The central slogan is brutally simple: MORE!

Some of us, Peter Harper noted in his Schumacher Lecture at Bristol in 2001, have apocalyptic visions of uncontrollable catastrophes in the future resulting from indiscriminate economic activity. He, as an optimist, and from his own experience as an environmental activist, has a different expectation. He thinks that as life gradually gets worse for everyone else, the Deep Greens (the people he calls the recessive genes of the sustainability movement) will be found to have solved what he calls the great riddle of reconciling modernity and sustainability: 'They will quite visibly be having a good time: comfortable, with varied lives and less stress, healthy and fit, having rediscovered the elementary virtues of restraint and balance.'

Twenty-five years of offering environmental choices to fellow citizens who came to the Centre for Alternative Technology with a variety of motives have led Peter Harper to adopt his relaxed approach to the task of convincing us all that our lifestyles have to change. Murray Bookchin would probably react differently, but many years earlier he posed the same issues in discussing the nature of a liberatory technology, one which frees rather than enslaves us. Can we imagine, he asked, that an ecologically viable economy could be based on a centralized nation state and its bureaucratic apparatus? He urged that, from the standpoint of the viability of the planet and all living things on it, anarchist concepts are not merely desirable, they are necessary:

> What was once regarded as impractical and visionary has now become eminently practical . . . If community face-to-face democracy, a humanistic, liberatory technology, and decentralisation are conceived of merely as reactions to the prevailing state of affairs – a vigorous 'nay' to the 'yes' of what exists today – a compelling, objective case can be made for the practicability of an anarchist society.

Environmental and ecological concerns have been advocated long enough for us to recognize peaks and troughs in the support they receive from the general, uncommitted public, whose involvement is vital for the manipulators of change. There are fashions in crisis-consciousness, as in most other aspects of our communal life. A comforting thought for anarchists is the reflection that a society advanced enough to accept the environmental imperatives of the

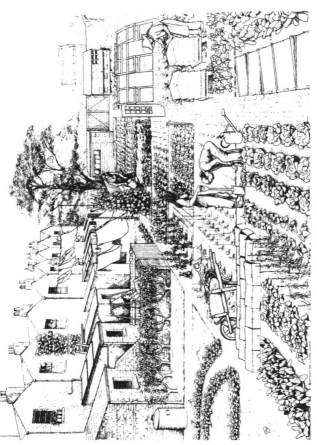

14. Community gardens, as envisaged by Clifford Harper.

21st century will be obliged to reinvent anarchism as a response to them.

For a very strong case has been made by such authors as Murray Bookchin and Alan Carter that anarchism is the only political ideology capable of addressing the challenges posed by our new green consciousness to the accepted range of political ideas. Anarchism becomes more and more relevant for the new century.

References

Chapter 1

Peter Marshall (ed.), *The Anarchist Writings of William Godwin* (London: Freedom Press, 1986)

Stewart Edwards (ed.), *Selected Writings of Pierre-Joseph Proudhon* (London: Macmillan, 1969)

K. J. Kenafick (ed.), *Marxism, Freedom and the State* (London: Freedom Press, 1984)

Paul Avrich (ed.), *The Conquest of Bread* (London: Allen Lane, 1972 [1892])

Colin Ward (ed.), *Fields, Factories and Workshops* (London: Allen and Unwin, 1974; London: Freedom Press, 1985 [1899])

John Hewetson (ed.), *Mutual Aid: A Factor of Evolution* (London: Freedom Press, 1987 [1902])

The passage quoted from Landauer is from Martin Buber, *Paths in Utopia* (London: Routledge and Kegan Paul, 1949).

F. G. Notehelfer, *Kotuku Shusui: Portrait of a Japanese Radical* (Cambridge: Cambridge University Press, 1971)

Robert A. Scalapino and George T. Yu, *The Chinese Anarchist Movement* (Bristol: Drowned Rat Publications, 1985)

Hai Ki-Rak, *History of the Korean Anarchist Movement* (Tuega, Korea: Anarchist Publishing Committee, 1986)

Adi Doctor, *Anarchist Thought in India* (Bombay: Asia Publishing House, 1964)

Geoffrey Ostergaard and M. Currell, *The Gentle Anarchists* (Oxford: Clarendon Press, 1971)

Sam Mbah and I. E. Igarewey, *African Anarchism: The History of a Movement* (Tucson, Arizona: See Sharp Press, 1997)

For the extent of anarchist involvement in assassinations, see Charles Townshend, *Terrorism: A Very Short Introduction* (Oxford: Oxford University Press, 2002)

Kropotkin's article on anarchism for the 11th edition of the *Encyclopaedia Britannica* is reprinted in Peter Kropotkin, *Anarchism and Anarchist Communism* (London: Freedom Press, 1987)

Chapter 2

Thomas Paine, *Common Sense* (Harmondsworth: Penguin, 1971 [1776])

J. Varlet, quoted in George Woodcock, *Anarchism* (Harmondsworth: Penguin, 1963)

Paris Commune, cited in Woodcock *op. cit.*

John Womack, *Zapata and the Mexican Revolution* (London: Thames and Hudson, 1972)

John Ross, *The War Against Oblivion: The Zapatista Chronicles* (Monroe, Maine: Common Courage Press, 2000)

Sue Branford and Jan Rocha, *Cutting the Wire: The Story of the Landless Movement in Brazil* (London: Latin American Bureau, 2002)

Paul Avrich, *The Russian Anarchists* (New Jersey: Princeton University Press, 1967)

Carl Levy, 'Italian anarchism 1870–1926', in *For Anarchism: History, Theory and Practice*, ed. David Goodway (London: Routledge, 1989)

Gerald Brenan, *The Spanish Labyrinth* (Cambridge: Cambridge University Press, 1943).

Pierre Broué and Emile Témine, *The Revolution and the Civil War in Spain* (London: Faber, 1970)

Burnett Bolloten, *The Spanish Revolution* (Chapel Hill: University of North Carolina Press, 1979)

Noam Chomsky, *American Power and the New Mandarins* (New York: Random House, 1967)

S. Faure, cited in Vernon Richards, *Lessons of the Spanish Revolution* (London: Freedom Press, 1953; 3rd edn. 1983)

Chapter 3

M. Buber, 'Society and the State', in *World Review*, July 1951, reprinted in M. Buber, *Pointing the Way* (London: Routledge and Kegan Paul, 1957)

Colin Ward, *Social Policy: An Anarchist Response* (London: London School of Economics, 1996; Freedom Press, 2000)

James Burnham, *The Managerial Revolution* (Harmondsworth: Penguin, 1944)

Richard Koch and Ian Godden, *Managing Without Management* (London: Nicholas Brealey, 1996)

Pierre Guillet de Monthoux, *Action and Existence: Anarchism for Business Administration* (Chichester: John Wiley, 1983)

A. Herzen, *From the Other Shore* (London: Weidenfeld and Nicholson, 1956; Oxford: Oxford University Press, 1979)

Chapter 4

Avi Schlaim, in *The Guardian*, 29 March 2003

M. Buber, *Israel and Palestine* (London: East and West Library, 1952)

M. Bakunin, *God and the State*, in *Bakunin on Anarchy*, ed. Sam Dogloff (London: Allen and Unwin, 1973)

N. Walter, cited in Colin Ward, 'Fundamentalism', in *The Raven*, 27, Vol. 7, No. 3 (London: Freedom Press, 1994)

Malise Ruthven 'Phantoms of ideology' in *Times Literary Supplement*, 19 August 1994

R. Rocker, cited in W. J. Fishman, *East End Jewish Radicals 1875–1914* (London: Duckworth, 1975)

E. W. Said, *Culture and Imperialism* (London: Chatto and Windus, 1993)

Fatima Mernissi, *Women and Islam: An Historical and Theological Enquiry* (Oxford: Basil Blackwell, 1991)

Chapter 5

Peter Kropotkin, *In Russian and French Prisons* (New York: Schocken Books, 1971 [1887])

Alexander Berkman, *Prison Memoirs of an Anarchist* (New York: Schocken Books, 1970 [1912])

David Cayley, *The Expanding Prison: The Crisis in Crime and Punishment and the Search for Alternatives* (Toronto: Anansi, 1998)

David Downes, 'The Macho Penal Economy: Mass Incarceration in the United States. A European Perspective', Lecture at New York University, February 2000.

Errico Malatesta, in *Umanità Nova*, 2 September 1920, reprinted in V. Richards (ed.), *Errico Malatesta: His Life and Ideas* (London: Freedom Press, 1965)

David Waddington, on BBC Radio 4, 19 February 2003

Geoffrey Ostergaard, *The Tradition of Workers' Control*, ed. Brian Bamford (London: Freedom Press, 1997)

Paul Thompson, *Why William Morris Matters Today: Human Creativity and the Future World Environment* (London: William Morris Society, 1991)

Chapter 6

William Godwin, *An Enquiry Concerning Political Justice* (Harmondsworth: Penguin, 1976 [1793]); *Uncollected Writings* (1785–1822), eds J. W. Marken and B. R. Pollin (Gainsville, Florida: Scholars' Facsimiles, 1968)

Paul Goodman, *Compulsory Miseducation*, 2nd edn. (Harmondsworth: Penguin, 1971)

National Union of Teachers, *The Struggle for Education* (London: NUT, 1970)

Stephen Humphries, *Hooligans or Rebels? An Oral History of Working-Class Childhood and Youth 1889–1939* (Oxford: Basil Blackwell, 1981)

Philip Gardner, *The Lost Elementary Schools of Victorian England* (London: Croom Helm, 1984)

Paul Thompson, 'Basic Skills', in *New Society*, 6 December 1984

Francesco Ferrer, see Paul Avrich, *The Modern School Movement: Anarchism and Education in the United States* (New Jersey: Princeton University Press, 1980)

Michael Bakunin, *God and the State* (London: Freedom Press, 1910; New York: Dover, 1970)

Harry Rée, reported in *The Teacher*, 8 April 1972

H. M. Chief Inspector of Schools, interviewed in *The Times*, 1 February 1995, and reported in *The Times Educational Supplement*, 27 January 1995

Michael Smith, *The Libertarians and Education* (London: Allen and Unwin, 1983)

John Shotton, *No Master High or Low: Libertarian Education and Schooling 1890–1990* (Bristol: Libertarian Education, 1993)

Jonathan Croall, *Neill of Summerhill: The Permanent Rebel* (London: Routledge and Kegan Paul, 1983)

Jonathan Croall (ed.), *All the Best, Neill: Letters from Summerhill* (London: Andre Deutsch, 1974)

Chapter 7

Max Stirner, *The Ego and His Own*, tr. Steven Byington (New York: Libertarian Book Club, 1963 [1907])

James J. Martin, *Men Against the State* (Colorado Springs: Ralph Myles, 1970)

David DeLeon, *The American as Anarchist: Reflections on Indigenous Radicalism* (Baltimore: Johns Hopkins University Press, 1978)

Henry David Thoreau, in Carl Bode (ed.), *The Portable Thoreau* (Harmondsworth: Penguin, 1979)

Randolph Bourne, *War and the Intellectuals: Collected Essays 1915–1919* (New York: The Resistance Press, 1964)

Ammon Hennacy, *The Autobiography of a Catholic Anarchist* (New York: Catholic Worker Books, 1954)

Dorothy Day, *The Long Loneliness* (New York: Harper and Row, 1952)

Robert Paul Wolff, *In Defence of Anarchism* (New York: Harper Colophon, 1976)

Robert Nozick, *Anarchy, State and Utopia* (Oxford: Blackwell, 1974)

David Friedman, *The Machinery of Freedom* (New York: Harper, 1975)

Murray Rothbard, *For a New Liberty: The Libertarian Manifesto* (New York: Collier, 1978)

F. von Hayek, *The Road to Serfdom* (London: Routledge, 1944)

Paul Goodman, 'Politics within Limits', reprinted in Taylor Stoehr (ed.), *Crazy Hope and Finite Experience: Final Essays of Paul Goodman* (San Francisco: Jossey-Bass, 1994)

Chapter 8

Dwight Macdonald, 'Politics Past', in *Encounter*, April 1957

Emma Goldman, 'The Tragedy of Women's Emancipation', in *Anarchism and Other Essays* (New York: Dover, 1969 [1911])

Alex Comfort, More Joy: *A Lovemaking Companion to The Joy of Sex* (London: Quartet, 1973)

Charles Duff, *A Handbook on Hanging* (London: Freedom Press, 1965)

Rudolf de Jong, *Provos and Kabouters* (Buffalo, NY: Friends of Malatesta, no date)

Raoul Vaneigem, *The Revolution of Everyday Life*, rev. edn. (London: Rebel Press, 1983)

George Monbiot, *Captive State* (London: Macmillan, 2000)

Sean M. Sheehan, *Anarchism* (London: Reaktion Books, 2003)

Chapter 9

Pierre-Joseph Proudhon, *The Principle of Federation*, tr. Richard Vernon (Toronto: University of Toronto Press, 1979)

Edward Hyams, *Pierre-Joseph Proudhon* (London: John Murray, 1979)

Willem de Haan, *The Politics of Redress* (London: Unwin Hyman, 1990)

Arthur Lehning (ed.), *Bakunin: Selected Writings* (London: Jonathan Cape, 1973)

Martin Miller, *Kropotkin* (Chicago: University of Chicago Press, 1976)

Camillo Berneri, *Peter Kropotkin: His Federalist Ideas* (London: Freedom Press, 1942 [1922])

Peter Hall, *Cities of Tomorrow* (Oxford: Basil Blackwell, 1988)

Council of Europe, 'The Impact of the Completion of the Internal Market on Local and Regional Autonomy' (Council of Europe Studies and Texts, Series No.12, 1990)

Thom Holterman, 'A Free United Europe', in *The Raven*, 31, Vol. 8, No. 3 (London: Freedom Press, 1995)

Chapter 10

Amartya Sen, *Poverty and Famine* (Oxford: Oxford University Press, 1981)

Jac Smit *et al.*, *Urban Agriculture: Food, Jobs and Sustainable Cities* (New York: United Nations Development Programme, 1996)

Tim Lang, in Ken Worpole (ed.), *Richer Futures: Fashioning a New Politics* (London: Earthscan, 1999)

John Houghton, cited in *The Raven*, 43, Vol. 11, No. 3 (London: Freedom Press, 2001)

Murray Bookchin, *Post-Scarcity Anarchism* (London:Wildwood House 1974)

Peter Harper, interviewed in W. & D. Schwartz *Living Lightly: Travels in Post-Consumer Society* (Oxford: Jon Carpenter 1998), and 'Natural Technology', lecture to the Schumacher Society, Bristol 2001

Alan Carter, *A Radical Green Political Theory* (London: Routledge, 1999)

Further reading

An earlier interpreter of anarchism remarked that 'anarchism is like blotting-paper: it soaks up everything', and, like most political ideologies, it can be given a variety of emphases. Beyond the general histories described in the Foreword, there are several books I should mention, providing alternative or additional interpretations extending those explored in this volume.

Max Blechman (ed.), *Drunken Boat: Art, Rebellion, Anarchy* (Brooklyn, NY: Automedia; and Seattle, WA: Left Bank Books, 1984)

Murray Bookchin, *Post-Scarcity Anarchism* (London: Wildwood House, 1974)

Alan Carter, *A Radical Green Political Theory* (London: Routledge, 1999)

Howard J. Ehrlich (ed.), *Reinventing Anarchy, Again* (Edinburgh and San Francisco: AK Press, 1996)

Clifford Harper, *Anarchy: A Graphic Guide* (London: Camden Press, 1987)

George McKay (ed.), *DIY Culture: Party and Protest in Nineties Britain* (London: Verso, 1998)

Jon Purkis and James Bowen (eds), *Twenty-First Century Anarchism: Unorthodox Ideas for a New Millennium* (London: Cassell, 1997)

Sean M. Sheehan, *Anarchism* (London: Reaktion Books, 2003)

Index

Expand your collection of
VERY SHORT INTRODUCTIONS

Visit the
VERY SHORT
INTRODUCTIONS
Web site

www.oup.co.uk/vsi

➤ **Information** about all published titles

➤ News of **forthcoming books**

➤ **Extracts** from the books, including titles
not yet published

➤ **Reviews** and views

➤ **Links** to other **web sites** and main
OUP web page

➤ Information about **VSIs in translation**

➤ **Contact** the editors

➤ **Order** other **VSIs** on-line

BUDDHISM
A Very Short Introduction
Damien Keown

From its origin in India over two thousand years ago Buddhism has spread throughout Asia and is now exerting an increasing influence on western culture. In clear and straightforward language, and with the help of maps, diagrams and illustrations, this book explains how Buddhism began and how it evolved into its present-day form. The central teachings and practices are set out clearly, and keys topics such as karma and rebirth, meditation, ethics, and Buddhism in the West receive detailed coverage in separate chapters. The distinguishing features of the main schools – such as Tibetan and Zen Buddhism – are clearly explained. The book will be of interest to anyone seeking a sound basic understanding of Buddhism.

'Damien Keown's book is a readable and wonderfully lucid introduction to one of mankind's most beautiful, profound, and compelling systems of wisdom. His impressive powers of explanation help us to come to terms with a vital contemporary reality.'

Bryan Appleyard

www.oup.co.uk/vsi/buddhism

COSMOLOGY
A Very Short Introduction
Peter Coles

What happened in the Big Bang? How did galaxies form? Is the universe accelerating? What is 'dark matter'? What caused the ripples in the cosmic microwave background?

These are just some of the questions today's cosmologists are trying to answer. This book is an accesible and non-technical introduction to the history of cosmology and the latest developments in the field. It is the ideal starting point for anyone curious about the universe and how it began.

'A delightful and accesible introduction to modern cosmology'

Professor J. Silk, Oxford University

'a fast track through the history of our endlessly fascinating Universe, from then to now'

J. D. Barrow, Cambridge University

www.oup.co.uk/isbn/0-19-285416-X

INTELLIGENCE
A Very Short Introduction
Ian J. Deary

Ian J. Deary takes readers with no knowledge about the science of human intelligence to a stage where they can make informed judgements about some of the key questions about human mental activities. He discusses different types of intelligence, and what we know about how genes and the environment combine to cause these differences; he addresses their biological basis, and whether intelligence declines or increases as we grow older. He charts the discoveries that psychologists have made about how and why we vary in important aspects of our thinking powers.

'There has been no short, up to date and accurate book on the science of intelligence for many years now. This is that missing book. Deary's informal, story-telling style will engage readers, but it does not in any way compromise the scientific seriousness of the book . . . excellent.'

Linda Gottfredson, University of Delaware

'Ian Deary is a world-class leader in research on intelligence and he has written a world-class introduction to the field . . . This is a marvellous introduction to an exciting area of research.'

Robert Plomin, University of London

www.oup.co.uk/isbn/0-19-289321-1